TESTED!

How we refused to let epilepsy define who we are

Margaret Hope and Anoush Hope-Fischer

ACKNOWLEDGEMENTS

We are grateful to our editor Mr. Carl Moore and associate editors, the Hon. George Lamming, Mrs. Sonia Mills and Dr. Patricia Rodney; to our readers Sir Woodville Marshall, Sir Henry Fraser, the former Prime Minister of Jamaica, the Hon P.J. Patterson and Prime Minister of Barbados, the Rt. Hon Freundel Stuart, Mrs. Selma James, Mr. Bruce Carter, Mrs. Nina Lopez, Mr. Sam Weinstein, Mrs. Halda Davis-Woodroffe, Mrs. Marva Griffith and Mr. Ian Archer. We are also grateful to Mr. Carl Moore for the perceptive Foreword, Sir Henry Fraser for the learned Introduction and Dr. Pat Rodney for the compassionate Postscript. Acknowledgements go also to photographers Messrs. Alric Gaskin, Gordon Brooks, Willie Alleyne, Kemal Layne, Brian Griffith, Dominic Davis, Pierce Tappin and Dr. Patricia Rodney and the unknown photographers who took the photos of our ancestors. We also wish to thank Mr. Curtis Challenor of Genesis Graphics for the Cover design and typesetting.

DEDICATION

We dedicate this book to son and brother Achebe; to husbands Christian and the late Chamberlain Colin Hope; granddaughter and daughter Isabella, and grandchildren, nieces, nephews and cousins, Frantz, Gaea, Dominic, Danielle, Jasmine, Jayden, Ayden and Nathan, who in the case of the husbands took care of us with our affliction. We thank God that siblings, cousins and grandchildren seem not to have inherited the gene.

ISBN: 978-976-95887-0-7

Published in Barbados

CONTENTS

INTRODUCTION

This dual autobiographical work is a wonderful, courageous memoir by a mother and daughter of the challenges of living with epilepsy. In the always lucid, often elegant prose of two professional writers, their story makes compelling reading. I read each volume at a single sitting, not even pausing for a drink!

Epilepsy (also known as epileptic seizures, seizure disorder, or more colloquially as "fits") is a common neurological problem. It comes fourth after migraine (by far the most common), strokes and Alzheimer's. Its prevalence is about one per cent in developed countries, but rather more in developing countries because of a higher frequency of birth trauma.

Seizure disorders manifest themselves in many different forms. The classic, dramatic and terrifying to witness form is the "grand mal" seizure with loss of consciousness, jerking of the limbs, frothing at the mouth, and sometimes tongue-biting and loss of urine. But there are many other lesser, though troubling forms. Many children have it only in infancy, teenagers may outgrow it as adults, while adults may develop the disorder at older ages due to developing a new disorder of the brain.

In my professional practice, as an internist/physician specialist at the Queen Elizabeth Hospital for more than 30 years, I found epilepsy the most challenging medical problem facing patients, doctors and other care-givers in Barbados. When I returned home in 1977 both public and medical attitudes to epilepsy were fossilised. The only medications available were the standard three drugs of the previous many decades, and the stigma associated with epilepsy was soul destroying. The two most important newer drugs were either not available or not used for epilepsy.

Let me illustrate this. Carbamazepine (innovator or trade name Tegretol) had been around for 20 years, but was considered only useful for a fairly rare condition called trigeminal neuralgia – episodic pain in the face. It is in fact one of the most valuable of all epilepsy drugs. And Valproate (innovator or trade name Epilim) was being used in Britain in the early 1970s with great success, but had not yet been introduced in Barbados.

I was fortunate in working as a resident physician at the Institute of Neurology in London in 1972 when it was undergoing clinical trials, and so I had experience with it. Also, during my postgraduate training and PhD work, I had the task of setting up a Therapeutic Drug Monitoring programme at the Royal Postgraduate Medical School. This was one of the first projects for measuring levels of the drug in the blood, so that doses could be titrated in each patient to produce the best results. Doses of these drugs vary from patient to patient depending on how they metabolise the drug. Each drug was shown to have a best therapeutic range, at which fits could be controlled, but not in such high doses as to produce unpleasant side effects of the kind described by Margaret and Anoush. The introduction of these two drugs, through the Barbados Drug Service and the National Formulary and setting up a Drug Monitoring lab at the QEH transformed the lives of many of our patients.

The next step was to persuade the Drug Service that epilepsy MUST be treated as one of the burdensome and costly-to-treat chronic conditions, so that the drugs would be included in the Drug Benefit Service, like those for high blood pressure and diabetes. And then there was the issue of doctor, patient and public education. It is often difficult to teach old dogs new tricks, and this applies to both patients and doctors. Since these times several very good additional epilepsy medications have become available. And in specialised centres in developed countries there are highly effective and safe neurosurgical procedures that can control seizure disorders in those relatively few patients who cannot be satisfactorily suppressed by correct use of medications.

Epilepsy management requires enormous patience on the part of doctors, and trust on the part of patients. It also requires that doctors take advantage of continuing medical education to update their practice, and it pains me to say that many of our doctors would not do that, did not use the better drugs, and would not accept that by measuring blood levels of the drug they could more frequently "get things right". The unpleasant side effects, especially the memory impairment and the gum problems that Margaret describes, are rarely a problem with careful management.

And few physicians–with so many problems to understand and manage, pay enough attention to epilepsy to counsel patients about learning their trigger factors. There are many of these. They range from sleep deprivation, hunger, glare and psychedelic lights, alcohol (even modest consumption in some people, not just withdrawal after a binge) and stress. People keep diaries of their appointments, their gym programmes, their dates, their finances and many other things. Why not their medical condition? But when all is said and done, the most common reason for having recurrent fits is poor compliance with taking medication as I shall discuss below.

Patients also, because of the stigma attached to the problem that is so graphically described by Margaret and Anoush, feel "different" and unhappy about having to take medication every day. This is ironic for two reasons: Firstly, when patients are told they have chronic life-shortening conditions (unless treated with daily medications) such as high blood pressure or diabetes, few object or feel stigmatised. Secondly, many patients and the general population happily every day take supplements and vitamins and complementary products (of very doubtful benefit, and costly to boot)!

Because of the embarrassment, compliance is a MAJOR, MAJOR problem. Many people with epilepsy compound the problem by omitting tablets or stopping them–for a huge variety of reasons, and this is the most common reason for the next fit. I recall one young lady whose fits had been well controlled for several years, but stopped her tablets the day before flying to New York, because she did not want her hosts to know she had epilepsy. She had a rebound grand mal fit in the car 36 hours later, and spent three days in a New York hospital, at the cost of almost her year's salary.

Epilepsy is a challenging condition, and its severity ranges from mild and generally innocuous, occasional seizures, of which there are many types, to the more frequent, severe ones that are difficult to control even by the specialist neurologist. Margaret and Anoush fall in that middle range, and they have coped remarkably well, given the difficulties most doctors, friends and family have in understanding and coping with this disorder. Their stories are told with great candour and courage, and should resonate with many hundreds of others with epilepsy.

Throughout these notes I have never used the term epileptic. It is a pejorative or negative term, as antiquated as the pit toilet! Patients should be able to say that they have a seizure disorder with the same candour, and without prejudice, as if they were saying that they have high blood pressure or diabetes, and therefore needing long-term regular medication.

Once again, I congratulate my friends Margaret and Anoush for having the courage to tell their stories so eloquently, so movingly and so compellingly. I believe they should be read by every one of our physicians, health care givers, teachers (who so often have to assist pupils who haven't taken their tablets), patients and relatives.

Professor Emeritus Sir Henry Fraser, K.A., MBBS, PhD, FACP, FRCP.

FOREWORD

A re you acquainted with someone who has a physical disability – perhaps they're minus the use of an arm or a leg, or maybe they're blind? Do you feel sorry for them – or do they feel sorry for you? Probably they lead normal lives – or as normal as circumstances will permit.

I accepted Margaret's invitation to write this Foreword with not a little trepidation. For one thing, I had only a passing acquaintance with the genetic condition that both she and her daughter inherited from their ancestors. And that acquaintance came about some 55 years ago when Margaret and I worked at our first jobs at *The Barbados Advocate*.

It was frightening when our proof-reader colleague Curtis Hinds suffered an attack. Only another colleague, sports reporter Don Norville, seemed to know what to do.

I never knew Margaret, too, was epileptic – not until she asked me to edit and proof-read this gripping story she calls *Tested*.

As I began to draft this I remembered a magazine given to me by my late barber Ken Williams with a short story by author Frank Skully. It is from a 1952 article titled "We licked our handicap" that I borrowed a few of Mr. Scully's observations about living with a disability. Back there in the 50s, before the euphemism entered the lexicon, it was okay to refer to a disability as a "handicap".

Skully's account aligns with the story that Margaret and Anoush relate in this gripping little book. They might not have "licked" their disability, but they have come close to doing just that. Both mother and daughter evoke a refreshing acceptance of their condition and demonstrate how every individual has to play the hand dealt to them.

With amazing candour, Margaret applies the journalism skills she learned as a junior reporter at *The Barbados Advocate* newspaper, while Anoush, the artist, applies deft strokes without air-brushing away any of the uncomfortable aspects of this malady. Her account of the numerous types of medication developed to help those afflicted with this disease is encyclopaedic.

Margaret dips copiously into her family's background, citing its proximity to the Barbadian plantocracy and her love of literature through the nurture and tutelage of her revered journalist grandfather Charles Bransway Rock. (She has written another short book about him titled *The Smell of Printer's Ink*).

She takes the reader on a vivid odyssey through early childhood, growing up at Haggatt's Plantation, her first job, her sojourn in England, where she met and was mentored by the legendary C.L.R. James and his wife Selma, her marriage and children, and her acceptance of epilepsy as she arrives at the autumn of her years, with far fewer occurrences.

Daughter Anoush is equally accepting of the condition which she treats as more of a humbug to be got around than the disability that it is. Indeed, she has taken on the role of activist against epilepsy.

She testifies: "My aim is to present this life-long experience to help families, care-givers, teachers, friends, co-workers, neighbours and the wider community to understand and appreciate the challenges that persons living with epilepsy face as they struggle through childhood and adolescence, learn to love and strive for independence and self-determination in adulthood."

This book is worthy of a place of prominence in your collection and of the widest circulation possible. I enjoyed working on it with these two strong Barbadian ladies.

Their message gives credence to the proverbial adage: "When life gives you lemons, make lemonade."

Carl Moore

Margaret Hope SCM, member of Writers Ink Inc., was born on Barbados in 1943. A journalist in Barbados and the Commonwealth of the Bahamas, she reached the top of her career as Editor of **The People** *newspaper in the early 70s. She served as a staff member of the Barbados Government Information Service for 31 years in many technical and administrative capacities. For 18 of those years she was Chief Information Officer in which capacity she worked as a film and video director, producer and script-writer and publisher. During that period she undertook a cne-year assignment as a UNESCO consultant with the CARICOM Secretariat in 1976 and in the mid-eighties she was seconded for two years as Public Relations Manager of the Board of Tourism. After her retirement from the public service in 2003, she was employed as Chief Executive Officer of the charity the Arnott Cato Foundation until her retirement in 2014. She is the author of a book of poetry* **To Be As Trees.** *She is the mother of two and grandmother of six.*

CHAPTER 1

HOW WE REFUSED TO LET EPILEPSY DEFINE WHO WE ARE

Barbados, my home where I lived continuously until 1963, is described in song as "The gem of the Caribbean Sea". A small country, a mere 166 square miles washed by the tortuous white-crested Atlantic Ocean, it recorded a population of 284,758 at the last census.

With its predominantly black population, a small white and mixed, (passing as we say) and even smaller Hindu and Muslim population, the country had a highly class-stratified history born out of slavery and colonialism dominated by the production of sugar which for centuries shaped its history, culture and social relations. Today, sugar has given way to tourism (where visitors, double the numbers of the population, visit our shores annually), the international financial sector, non-sugar agriculture, the manufacturing sector and a most uncreative retail sector.

A riot in 1937 became the catalyst for the reformation of the society with, a few years later, the creation of a mass-based political party, the Barbados Labour Party, headed by Grantley Adams, a black middle-class Oxford-trained lawyer and the formation of its sister organisation, the Barbados Workers' Union. This development was followed by self-rule with Adams becoming the first Premier and the entire population of adults earning the right to vote. Thus began the process of democratisation and the reins of power being firmly grasped by representatives of the black population, although, as is the case still today, the small white population continues to control the economy.

The Barbados Labour Party's reign of power came to an end in 1961 when a London School of Economics economist, and London-trained lawyer, Errol Barrow, who had earlier broken with Adams and formed his own party, the Democratic Labour Party, took power, and led the country into independence in 1966 and became the island's first Prime Minister.

Barrow was an ex-Royal Air Force navigator, an excellent cook and sailor and was, like his uncle Charles Duncan O'Neal, a charismatic leader with a clear social democratic vision for Barbados. Among other things he introduced free primary to tertiary education transforming the landscape of the society. This produced a solid black middle-class which, up to then, was small and mainly professional or public servants who were able to afford to pay for education at all levels for their off-spring. He also introduced a social security scheme and equal pay for men and women.

Born in 1943, two years before the birth of the mass political party and two years after the birth of the trade union movement, I grew up in a Barbados which was undergoing this transformation of its social, political and economic history, which renders it, even today, as one of the most developed countries in the developing world as assessed by the United Nations.

My name is Margaret Carter Hope. I am an epileptic.

I believe once an epileptic always an epileptic, although I have not had a grand seizure for 51 years and have been free of any kind of mild episode for 21. My daughter Anoush differs. She claims that she is a person who has epilepsy but is not epileptic. This memoir of a mother and daughter with epilepsy offers different perspectives and we leave the reader to draw their own conclusion but to reach one conclusion that disability does not mean inability.

The derelict structure of my grandparents' home in Watt's Village.

I grew up in a wooden and concrete bungalow, nestled among an orchard of banana, golden apple, ackee, guava and sugar apple trees in Watt's Village, St. George, Barbados. The house was situated in a village, a few buildings down from my paternal grandfather's imposing home of "wall" (stone) house and shop which towered over the village.

My grandparents, Johnny and Louise Carter, had lived there all their married lives and there my father Julian Estwick Carter, better known as "Erie", and his six older siblings were born and grew up. Most of my early life as an epileptic is shrouded in the fog, caused in part by time and in part by a very poor memory which seems to be a condition common among epileptics.

My mother Joyce told me that I had my first convulsion on August 9, 1943, when I was three days old, the date coincidentally when three years later she was to give birth to her premature seven-month baby boy.

My Mum said I had seizures at three- to four-month intervals for most of my childhood. In fact, after I was a teenager, one evening I was telling her that a friend had told me that day that I was painfully thin. She comforted me by telling me that although I was thin I had beautifully shaped limbs and the skin colour of a beautiful ripe dounce, and added, "People can be cruel. Imagine when I was a young mother, one doctor, a family friend, told me 'Why you don't leave the child in peace and let her die? You have two other healthy children'."

Johnny Carter (Grandad), Louise, his wife, and "G", their only daughter

I vaguely remember my first five years at Watt's Village.

I remember Sonny Boy our "yard boy" picking toy bucketsful of ackees for us children to suck until our tongues were too sore to eat. Sonny Boy was a teenaged member of staff who did odd jobs, supervised outdoor play of the children and fed and watered the chickens, among other chores suitable for his 15 years. The title of "yard boy" was given to such persons working in plantation yards or homes and today my Sonny Boy, now 87 and a retired security guard in New York, still chats with me for two or three hours every Christmas day before he goes to join his wife who is in a nursing home and before taking her over to spend the day with their daughter, a New York financier.

Margaret and Diane in 1950

I remember the long walks with our nurse-maids through the village with our cousins Carlisle, Ronnie, Cicely, Claire and Janice.

I remember going down to Martin's Bay in the car to visit my beloved grumpy grandfather and his adopted daughter to spend the weekend swimming and catching crabs and drinking goat's milk, brimming with the oil of the cocoa.

At Martin's Bay I remember Tom the fisherman who lived in a simple unpainted one-room house set on a little hill. Tom was a poor white or "eckybecky", as poor whites were called, with the bluest eyes and who, as gently as he tended his chickens and his catch, taught us things about shells, fish and the treacherous and beguiling water of Martin's Bay.

When it rained and the water gushed down the drains running along the side of the road at Watt's Village, with "Ol' man river" playing softly in the background on the radio, we sat with envy, looking through the window at the children of the village – a few boys and even fewer daring girls – racing their paper boats in the rushing water with much joy, shouts and laughter.

There were four of us. I was the eldest of the three children. I was tall, dark and skinny. Indeed, so skinny that my father's nicknames for me were "Pings" – the sound of two knitting needles banging together – and "Fine Twine".

Diane, my plump disgustingly healthy sister, fair, with grey eyes and auburn hair, nicknamed by our father "Ginger", was a year younger, and Bruce, my baby brother, was three years younger. Bruce, who had been a sickly premature baby, had grown into a healthy toddler and adult until he reached midlife when he developed cluster headaches.

And there was Woodie our cousin (Woodbine Davis), swarthy skin with coiled back hair, a handsome face and the most placid, easy-going personality I have ever come across in my 72 years. He was like an older brother and he too had his special names for us: I was "Mags", Diane was "Deegs" and Bruce was "Bounce".

My father was a planter who had joined that profession at Ridge Plantation at aged 19 as a junior overseer after graduating from Combermere School. He lived on the property where he worked. However, he was no longer in residence, when we lived at Watt's Village. I remember he played cricket every Saturday and I can still see him in his white shirt and pants eating his puddin' 'n' souse and then off he would go.

Erie Carter

13

Once a month, at night, he dressed up in a dark suit and went out to the meeting of the Masonic Lodge, something I learned only later, since the trip, to our young minds, seemed shrouded in mystery, for he never spoke of it when questioned.

When I was six, the plantation built a modern duplex on its grounds. The larger section of the house was allocated to the senior overseer, my father, and the other section, to the junior overseer. We moved into this spanking new home with joy and spent many days playing in the tracks between the cane fields, flying kites, playing tag, and the other games that children get up to in the Caribbean; like hop scotch and pitching marbles, often joined by other children visiting with their parents who clearly enjoyed playing in the great outdoors.

I don't remember getting convulsions at the Ridge although my mother said I had them often and Diane confirmed this and said when they occurred she would go behind the bed and cry and once got spanked because it was thought she was laughing at me.

What I do remember, is playing one day with paper and twine wrapped around my feet, in imitation of a pair of slippers my mother wore, when a kitten playing with the twine, scratched a pimple on my ankle and blood-poisoned me. Aunt Celeste Smith moved in with us to nurse me and Dr. "Puppy" Ward came every day to supervise the administering of injections every two hours for two weeks. I survived but even today when I am very tired the spot on my ankle hurts.

Because of my epilepsy I went to school not as often as I should have and my mother taught me at home and that created a bond. I can still conjure up her image and find solace from her imagined presence, when distressed.

My mother, Joyce Carter née Rock, was considered one of the most beautiful women in Barbados and she knew it and dressed the part, making many of her own clothes: simple square-necked shifts which flattered her voluptuous body which was almost all leg.

When she went to cricket in her wide-brim hats there were few who could match her style. Among those were Mrs. Gloria Goddard, wife of the white captain of the West Indies team John Goddard, Mrs. Cece Gittens, the wife of a cricket commentator and teacher Mr. Stanton Gittens, and Mrs. Hyacinth Burton, later Lady Burton and the wife of Permanent Secretary Sir Carlisle

Burton. For special occasions my mother's clothes were made by one of the island's finest seamstresses, Mrs. Elsie Gay, who was married to my father's sister, Aunt G's eldest son Fred Gay.

Mum was a housewife. She was always busy in the kitchen, in the yard, teaching the Barbadian cooks on staff pepper pot and other dishes she had learned in British Guiana. She had grown up there and as a teenager managed my grandfather's household. My siblings confirmed later and agreed that we all thought she was born with lipstick on

Joyce Carter

and her hair combed, since we never saw her dishevelled or in a night gown. She was to go to work for the first time at the age of 40, at the Southern District Council, joining a few middle-class and white Barbadian women who had chosen to work in midlife having been housewives all their young married lives.

As a child, I loved to watch her dress and fix her face and I used to scotch beside her to observe. I still own the dressing table bench of mahogany which she had had built so that I could sit comfortably next to her while she dressed.

My mother was born in Belle Gully, St. Michael, in a simple stone house. Her father, Charles Bransway Rock, the son of a red hair Irish train driver, was a Pitman's shorthand gold medalist, teacher and entrepreneur who had reported the interviews for the Moyne Commission during the investigation of the 1937 riots in the English-speaking Caribbean. He carried the initials FIPS (Fellow of the Pitman's Society) after his name. Barbadian historian F.A Hoyos, writing about Granddad in his book about Sir Grantley Adams, *The Quiet Revolutionary*, on page 66, said: "Charlie Rock made frequent, if somewhat mysterious, appearances in the reporters' room, for he was not a member of *The Advocate* staff.

He was the official reporter of the Legislative Council and since *Hansard* was produced by *The Advocate* printers he was cordially welcomed as an honorary member of the reporters' room. He seemed to love the smell of printer's ink and we benefited immeasurably from his presence. He had lived and

Charles Bransway Rock

worked as a journalist in British Guiana and Bermuda and was a man of wide and deep knowledge.

I was particularly grateful for the special attention and help he gave me as a youngster in the profession."

My grandmother, Alma Rock, née Storey, from whom my sister inherited her grey eyes, died when my mother was three years old. Granddad married again, to a Guyanese poet, Florence Chabral. Mother's stepmother knew little of children and would send her upstairs of the Bay Street home to get her shoes in the dark, leaving my mother with a permanent fear of the dark. All her adult life she slept with a light on in her bedroom or the adjacent room. After his second marriage Grandad emigrated with his wife and daughter to British Guiana where he continued his journalism part-time but became an entrepreneur, opening a laundry – The Black Cat. Mummy went to school at the Convent in Georgetown.

At 18 she returned to Barbados, which she used to visit on her holidays, to stay with the Bohnes, her life-long friends of Cynthia, Dolly and Carl; the first two who were godmothers to Diane and me, respectively. Aunt Cynthia was married to a pharmacist, Lyte Hutson, and they had two children, Hewley and Margot. Aunt Dolly married in late life to Cyril Payne, the owner of Harrow Plantation, had two daughters, Janice and Jennifer. Carl died when I was about 15 in an airplane accident when the plane hit turbulence and he broke his neck.

From Westbury Road, where Mummy and Granddad then lived on their return to Barbados, she became the second wife of my father, 12 years older, and thus began her life as a married woman.

CHAPTER 2

HAGGATT'S

Derelict Haggatt's plantation house

Around 1950 my father was hired as manager of Haggatt's Plantation, and we moved to St. Andrew and the stately home with its large rooms and polished wooden floors, lofty windows and a foyer where my parents played bridge almost every weekend with the Bannisters from Morgan Lewis Plantation and where we all would go on alternate weekends. This was one of the sites for the 1957 filming of *Island In The Sun*, and all the girls, including me, fell in love with Harry Belafonte, while all the males fell in love with Dorothy Dandridge.

To a child, Haggatt's was like a gem nestling in the palm of God. It was surrounded by hills and fields of cane and was a stone's throw by car from the sand dunes of Lakes with its hostile sea and waterways where wild birds congregated in the winter months of North America. We would go there on weekends and holidays with the dogs running at the side of the car, and swim mostly in the shoal, and pick fat porks and cashews, which grew wild on the sand dunes.

John Peterkin, the 15-year-old son of the factory manager, would go with us and shoot wild birds and roast them. They were delicious to children who were too picky to eat rabbit at home. In fact, Mummy had to put chicken wings and legs in the rabbit stew to trick us into eating it. With John, we would also climb the hills surrounding the plantation and catch crayfish in the river running through the property. John and Woodie became very close and we would simply traipsed around behind them till they grew tired of us and banished us for a nap.

A highlight of our stay there was the visit of friends and relatives from town to spend the day, or from neighbouring plantations, eating lunches of baked chicken and duck, baked pork covered in crispy hard skin, stewed rabbit and ham, which my mother made in a very scientific process of injections and rubbing salts and placed in incubators. There were also the usual starches of macaroni, yam and sweet potato pies, potato salad, boiled corn and peas and rice and vegetables. We would play cricket–boys and girls, children and adults and the yard staff. Everybody was conscripted to make up the two teams.

The Peterkins left Haggatt's and Louis Webster came to live in the factory house taking over as manager. He was accompanied by his wife, Sis, and his two children, Margot and three-year-old Jimmy, who became attached to me and I to them, Jimmy in particular. One day Jimmy came over to the plantation house in a flood of tears. I asked him what was wrong and in his baby language he said "Gaget," –he couldn't say Margaret–"Mummy said I can't marry you!" He was three and I was 11 years older.

Neither of us understood what she meant but she had managed to convey to me that there was a fundamental difference between people like Jimmy and people like me, which had never occurred to me. Despite this comment her attitude to me did not change and when Jill Webster, Louis's niece, came to visit she too became my friend, a friendship that lasted into our teens when we both modelled for *The Advocate*, where I was later employed.

I had been told on my return to Barbados in 1972 that the Websters had all gone to Canada to live. However, my editor Carl stirred curiosity in me as to what had happened to my Jimmy and I asked a Barbadian historian after this book was completed if he knew Jill and Jimmy Webster. He pointed me to them. At the age of 61 a slim, handsome Jimmy, a semi-retired electronics specialist who had worked mainly in Canada and Europe and Jill, now 72, and a former pantomime producer whose work I had enjoyed without connecting her to it, spent a morning with me combing over old newspapers looking for evidence of our "beautiful youth", while Jimmy photographed what we found.

Let me go back in time. It was in my ninth year that I had the first convulsion that I remember as clearly today as if it had happened only this morning.

The day that I had the first convulsion that I remember followed a Sunday when the Smiths visited for the day. Aunt Celeste, the nurse who ministered to me when I had the cat scratch, was accompanied by her husband, Uncle Col, and their three children – Ethel, Philip and Wendell. Wendell was a chubby solemn child, who would become one of Barbados's most celebrated comedians and actors. We had played cricket and when they left at dusk I fell into bed tired from roaming the plantation and the lively game of cricket.

The next day was a normal day: we went to school at the Belleplaine Elementary School, came home and had dinner. Dinner was an early affair on the plantation to meet the hunger needs of Daddy when he came in from riding his horse around the plantation shaded from the sun by his cork hat with his whip laid across his horse's back, more for decoration than function.

After dinner Mummy suggested that we go for a walk. We went through the office door and walked along the lane which ran next door to the house, past the overseer's quarters and into the bushy area on both sides of the path planted with green pea trees. We started picking peas, shelling the baby soft ones and eating them.

I remember feeling disoriented and unable to focus. I tapped my forehead a few times to clear my head and to regain focus. My stomach was upset and the sky was spinning. The next thing I knew I was lying in my mother's bed in pajamas with a blinding headache.

Mummy told me that I had had a convulsion while we were out walking. She said I had fallen and had had a fit. She told me she had broken off piece of the branch of the pea tree to put between my teeth and tongue and after the fit I had lapsed into an unconscious state. She said she and Woodie had brought me back to the house where I had slept for three hours. I told her my head was hurting and she wrapped it in a cloth soaked in Limacol, a lime-scented water, which I learned to dislike because it reminded me of illness. She said it was no different from the many I had had over the years, except this time I didn't vomit.

This was the first time I remembered what had led up to the fit, the aura, as my neurologist calls it. But it was to repeat itself many times at elementary school, and at the Alleyne Secondary School.

At elementary school the children were cruel. "Don't let the fitsy white girl touch the ball; she has the devil and she will give him to us." Because we lived on the plantation we were not considered white but were called the white children at school and fairs, although many of the children were fairer skinned than Bruce and me. But in those days before free secondary education, which transformed Barbados and the class structure, class and colour were often substituted. This was compounded by the plantation system where black people who assumed the position of head of the plantation – the preserve of the white people – were deemed white.

The children were more compassionate at Alleyne and I was not tormented, but then, I had a cousin who was a senior teacher at the school and who boarded with us at that time. Mummy kept me at home after a convulsion so I missed a lot of school but my grandfather kept me supplied with all the classics and whenever they were looking for me I could be found sitting in a chair before the bookcase. In high school Diane and Bruce were boarded out; Woodie, who by this time was studying to be a solicitor, spent most of the time in the Belle Gully with his father. Mummy and I grew even closer.

Life at Haggatt's was the dawning of the consciousness of my spiritual and religious self. For a few years I switched between Jehovah's Witness, Anglican – the predominant religion, since I went to church regularly at St. Andrew's Parish Church (where the Reverend Edward Gatherer presided after which he would visit us at the plantation), Church of God and Seventh Day Adventist. These conversions occurred as one or other of the household staff – washer, cleaner or cook – got hold of me to convert me. The one thing all of them agreed on was that I was blessed and lucky because God protected me, since I did not get seriously hurt with a dangerous fall as I gallivanted all over Haggatt's.

And this belief that God protected me, fed by their faith, gave me a strong belief in God. It was such a constant presence that later in life when I had my depressions they always took the form of a religious phenomenon which I remember clearly, reading the Bible and writing down on paper the names of persons I knew and their biblical counterparts and forecasting their futures.

But of all the staff, the one I loved best was Miss Murray, a tall, jet black, slim, middle-aged woman who looked, with her tightly drawn black hair, like the carvings I have seen in my trip to Africa. She had many children and told me many years later that many of them had gone to live in other Caribbean islands and had done very well. She had a dictum: "Believe in

God and gather yourself to yourself."

But soon the world of Jimmy Webster, Miss Murray and the plantation came to an end and we moved to Christ Church.

CHAPTER 3

THE SECOND REMEMBERED CONVULSION

When we moved to Christ Church in 1956, I transferred to Foundation Girls' School and, strangely enough, I became free of epilepsy, although I was told I had seizures at home, but infrequently.

I had a busy and exciting school and social life. By the time I reached Foundation the oligarchy had gotten rid of some of the black managers from the plantations and Daddy was one of them. Like some of the black managers, he wanted to buy a plantation in isolated Boscobel, St. Andrew much to my mother's horror.

She won that battle and we left St. Andrew. Bernard "Bree" St. John, later to become Prime Minister of Barbados and Sir Harold, after his knighthood, had made a higher offer but gave way to my father and we moved into "Brumaran" at Sargeant's Village, Christ Church. There I lived until I left for England in 1963 and to which I returned in 1966. I was to return to that house in the 70s as a single parent.

At school I was not allowed to play games or participate in plays, but, other than that, I participated in the choir, and all other activities. My poor memory continued to be a problem in school and I secretly revised my school work to keep up especially those subjects I loved and ended up excelling in English Language, English Literature and History.

Brumaran

I had two sets of friends, my class mates and my social friends. There were Daphne Williams, whose grandfather on her mother's side was a black doctor and whose father was a St. Lucian Indian and, Margot Gittens, who was a fair-skinned girl with black curly hair from the family types who got jobs in stores and banks because of their colour, long before blacks could hold such a job

There were other friends more social than school friends: Angela Elder, who boys said looked like me and who became Head Girl and was a peaceful, cheerful darling, and Margaret Evelyn, a little spitfire.

There were three other girls whom I was fairly close to because of family ties and who were a little younger: Andrea Gollop, a theatrical little person who lived in a nearby development and who was deeply loved by my mother; Amor Tappin, whose father Pierce was one of my father's best friends, and Jeanette Simmons, who used to go to the same parties and family get-togethers. Janet and I were bridesmaids at Monica Scott's wedding to a Canadian when we had walked in fancy blue dresses from the home of Parochial Treasurer in St. Philip, Pearson Scott, who was Monica's father, through the village, lined by villagers looking on, to St. Philip's Parish Church. There are too many to mention, but I must include Celia Hinds, a family friend whose claim to fame was that she read the dictionary as adolescent girls read romantic novels.

Daphne Williams and I were both writers who did very well in literature and always had note books filled with our work–poetry in my case–and short stories in hers. My love poems were very popular and young teachers like Miss Barker, the English teacher, used to select the ones they wanted to send their boyfriends abroad.

Socially, a group of us: Angela and Margaret, Anton Norris, Barbados's first medalist at the Commonwealth Games; a sometime back-sliding Closed Brethren member Lionel Barrow; Bunny Manning, a travel agent, and my sister Diane used to have get-togethers at the girls' homes, usually for puddin' 'n' souse, or go to young people's dances and private parties.

I was also close friends with my headmistress Enid Lynch's nephews, Neville and Hugh Millington, Ian Walters of Cable and Wireless and Vanburn Guiler, the son of the owner of Borne's Bay Rum, to whom I had become very close when we lived near to him for a short while between Haggatt's and the purchase of "Brumaran"–and remain so until this day–and Dru

Symmonds, whose father was the only black Barbadian owner of a bank in Barbados. Dru married Margot Hutson, the daughter of Aunt Cynthia and Uncle Lyte.

I must speak of Enid Lynch – Barbados scholar, leading educator and later, Senator. I was once feeling very sorry for myself one sports day because I could not run like my peers and told her so, as she leaned on a tree, her hands deep into her pockets. She made no comment. Two Saturdays later, she invited me to her home for tea. After tea, she led me into a room where I saw a big child crawling like a baby on the floor. It was her son who had suffered brain damage after being dropped as a baby by a helper. I never felt sorry for myself again.

The challenges of epilepsy – of feeling alone, depressed and fearful of when seizures would occur – were emotions which did not dog my teenage years, and although I was conscious of my vulnerability, I was a very friendly, self-confident, extroverted teenager with lots of friends but with a persistent spiritual inner life of reading, writing poetry in the study situated in the back gallery of the two-storey house in Sergeant's Village, inspired by my grandfather's tutelage and engaging in fierce debates with my friends and family, discussing all the problems of the world.

My grandfather had taught me to love literature and books and writing and I often read to him or discussed a book he had given me to read in the afternoons after school. He lived at the top of Oistins Hill in a house which Woodie Davis bought from my mother who had inherited it at my grand-father's death and which has remained with few changes in the excellent state it was when my granddad was alive.

The house was a short walk from Foundation Girls' School and I was sup-posed to be going for lessons in shorthand and typing. Invariably he would say I looked too tired to study and I would read to him or discuss books we had both read. I loved him and he used to say with love in his voice that I was the only ugly thing he had ever loved. The gentleness and love he poured on me was not extended to my siblings, or to anybody else, for that matter. My siblings still remember the Christmas lunches as a torture as he corrected their pronunciation of "Worcestershire", as in Worcester-shire sauce.

It was in Sargeant's Village that I first became aware that my father's solitary drinking in his youth on the plantation after his first wife died had turned him into a weekend alcoholic as he grew older. He was a Dr. Jekyll and Mr. Hyde who made not a sound from Monday to Friday as he sat reading in his favourite chair, silence broken only by the banging of his pipe into an ashtray at regular intervals. However, on weekends he talked non-stop from Saturday morning to Sunday night when he fell into a comatose sleep, not before declaring to all within earshot that "My life is an open book", from which I drew the working title of this book– *Frankly Speaking.*

He, it appeared, carried the epileptic gene since, when he got ill and had a high temperature, he had convulsions. His drinking was a bone of contention between him and my mother and in the later years they grew apart emotionally.

Daddy spent a great deal of time with his male planter friends like George Ward, of the legendary black Ward family, overseer Douglas Gay and Amor's Daddy, photographer Pierce Tappin. On the other hand Mummy grew closer to us children and especially to me, the vulnerable one. As a vulnerable one I became the one who kept her company at the cinema, especially the drive-in, which was a stone's throw from our home at the end of Sargeant's Village.

My mother's warm enveloping love was in the main responsible for me feeling normal and relaxed and accepting my epilepsy. She took me everywhere in the car yet I missed out on many rides into Bridgetown with friends in the bus and going to the cinema.

I remember the first time I was to ride in a bus; I was 15. I was going with Diane to visit my friend Daphne Williams at her parents' guest house, Crystal Waters, in Worthing. Diane protested. She didn't want to go with me in the bus and Mummy insisted. We entered the bus and she waited until I sat down and sat somewhere else. When we got back home, I complained and she said that she didn't want to sit with me because I would talk loudly as if I was in a car and I might get sick. But these episodes were few and far between.

Then the second attack that I remember with clarity occurred when I was 16 and we, as a family, had been invited to Basil Springer's 17th birthday party at the home of a relative of his, Permanent Secretary Fred Cozier, in Culloden Road.

Basil was the son of Charles and Rita Springer, and old middle-class family, whose uncle was to become Governor General of Barbados, Sir Hugh

Springer. The Springers were related to Errol Barrow, first Prime Minister of Barbados, the most distinguished to date, and who is now a national hero like Basil's uncle, Hugh.

On the day of Basil's party I awoke with excitement. I remember standing in front of the wardrobe and running my hand across the front of a blue and white lace and chiffon dress which was hanging there. It was a Saturday and Waithe our cook had prepared a dish of cou-cou and liver stew, a meal I normally enjoyed but was too excited to eat. I read fitfully until it was time to dress. When I thought it was time, I bathed, not in the shower but in a bucket in the bathroom warmed with hot water, for I was not allowed to shower as an epileptic. My mother was ever cautious. I dressed carefully and waited patiently for my parents and siblings to finish dressing. It had rained and we drove through streets shiny with rain water, down Collymore Rock to Culloden Road and the Cozier's home.

The living room was filled with young people and their parents and music was playing softly. After a drink, someone, I don't remember who, asked me to dance. I was a good dancer. That was my claim to fame and the good male dancers gravitated to me, transforming me into a magical figure as I got caught up in the music.

Tonight was different. As I danced I suddenly felt the room and its inhabitants receding and going out of focus. I asked to be allowed to sit and I remember nothing until I regained consciousness lying in my beautiful dress now rumpled and covered in vomit in a bed with my mother hovering. I had a blinding headache. I knew with a sinking feeling that in front of my friends I had had an epileptic fit.

"Are you feeling better?" my mother asked. I nodded; she said then, "Let us go home." I remember nothing of what would have been the humiliating walk out of the house to the car and the drive home. I, who had lived on phenobarbitone all my life so far, vowed I would never have another epileptic fit and promised myself that I would take the medication faithfully.

The aftermath of this teenaged humiliating attack was my feeling of getting another attack when I went out or to school. I also believed that my friends, who assured me it was all in my imagination, had changed towards me.

But the feeling clung for a while and I did not dance at parties with my usual gusto until we went to a Christmas Sea Scouts dance at almost eighteen when I got caught up in the magic of the evening, the frilly white dresses, the boys elegantly tailored and the wonderful music by a real band and forgot myself and relaxed in my dancing partner Lionel's arms.

CHAPTER 4

EPILEPSY THE THEORY

From the earliest times and times not so early, epileptics were believed to be possessed by devils and the seizure was the evidence of the devil leaving or entering the body of the epileptic. But apart from the aura – that sensation that you are losing focus and control – I have noted three things which I have never raised with a doctor. The first is that I am absent-minded; second, I have very poor memory and third, the mould of my head is very sensitive; so sensitive that if someone came and stood over my head unknown to me, I would feel the sensation of crawling in my mould and would turn around or look up.

The best example of the last one occurred one day when I was lying on the Pebbles Beach near the "hot pot" reading. I felt as if the skin on the "mould" of my head was shrinking. I jumped up and there was a big crab resting near where my head had been. My neurologist Dr. Sean Marquez had an MRI done of my brain and found no brain damage, which I found interesting, given the sensitivity of my fontanel or "mould."

The experts claim that there are five challenges of living with epilepsy. These are: social – you may feel like a burden and have social and cultural stigmas from others lacking in knowledge; emotional – you may feel isolated, embarrassed, depressed, out of control and fearful of when the next seizure will occur; professional – you may find it difficult to find a job, keep a job or work at certain occupations; financial – you may have fears about your financial security (lack of proper insurance coverage, etc.) and health – you may be more susceptible to physical injury from convulsions, falls and accidents. I was spared most of these challenges except the embarrassment, and in later life, the depressions and feelings of being out of control.

"There are two types of epileptic seizures: generalised and partial," writes Anne Scherer.

"A generalised seizure (the one I had up to 21) affects the whole brain, while partial affects only part of the brain.

"Generalised seizures are identified by 'absence', generally known as blanking, and convulsions and sudden jerking movements.

"Partial seizures cause twitching of the legs, arms, vision distortions and altered emotions, but the person remains conscious."

Some people also experience an aura – an unusual feeling in the stomach and a sense of fear or other sensory change before an observational seizure occurs. The aura is the beginning of a simple partial seizure which then spreads to involve a larger area of the brain.

In the case of the convulsions I remember I seem to combine both the generalised and the partial seizures since I get the aura, the upset stomach, the sense of fear, the sensory change which I described as the world going out of focus and I bang my head to clear it and bring it back in focus and then I move into the generalised seizure.

In my midlife I was to have the partial while asleep, and would only know I had had an episode when I woke up the next day with my tongue bitten up.

CHAPTER 5

JOURNALISM

I left school at 18, two years after my last attack at 16, and never had a recurrence until much later, but was constantly disconcerted by the fear of another seizure.

Two weeks after I left school, at my grandfather's suggestion, nay insistence, and armed with my poetry, I asked for and was granted an interview with the Managing Director of *The Advocate*, Dougal Smith, a tall, elegant, handsome New Zealander, who was representative of the English newspaper, *The Mirror*, which now owned that paper.

Mr. Smith asked me why I wanted to be a journalist and I told him for two reasons: my grandfather was a journalist and had educated me with highly selective reading to become a journalist, and I was a poet. I handed him my portfolio. He took his time reading the poems, as he must have read a love poem or two. He hired me on the spot as a social reporter but said I had to work as a general reporter for six months to hone my journalistic skills.

I worked at *The Advocate* until I left for London in 1963 and in that period had one major illness but not one attack of epilepsy, although I worked long hours and had a hectic life. However, at *The Advocate* I was afflicted by the crippling illness of rheumatoid arthritis at 18 when I was hospitalised for a lengthy period and had to be carried up the long stairs of the newspaper, basket style when I did return to work.

I believe I was the first black female journalist in Barbados. The only other female journalist on staff was a white Barbadian, Toni Browne, and later after I joined the staff, her mother, Ma Browne, joined the staff as Woman's Editor. Ma Browne was replaced by the beautiful brown-skinned Cyralene Fields. One of the original proprietors of *The Advocate*, who was still employed there as Editor, Ian Gale, fell deeply in love with her and later married her.

To me, *The Advocate* by day was a hectic place; my first assignment included covering hawkers complaining about vegetable wholesale prices. Dougal was always asking me questions about Bajan life and one day I confided in him that there was a rumour going the rounds that girls from Barclays Bank were taking their shorty pajamas to work and after work were going up to the Savannah where the white expatriate male bank staff lived and modelling for them.

The next day I came to work and saw the newspaper. I don't remember the headline, but the first paragraph invited parents of middle-class girls who worked at banks to search their hand bags before letting them leave home since they were … etc., etc. – suggesting that more than modelling occurred. I was very circumspect with Dougal Smith after that.

We would come back from our assignments and sit at a desk built in a semi-circle on the outskirts of the room and type our stories, hardly speaking, typewriters clattering until summoned by the News Editor or one of the big shots working in cubby holes or separate desks off in a corner. The sub-editors sat in the middle of the room around a horse-shoe-shaped desk.

Carl Moore

I loved best the evening when the clerical staff had gone home and the news room became the sea of raucous jokes and laughter and serious debate as the reporters and the sub-editors "put the paper to bed"

There was the granddad of the newsroom, Joe Broome, a boisterous hulk of a man with a booming voice that could be heard in the next street. There was Tony Vanterpool, the tall, brown-skinned News Editor (legendary Mitchie Hewitt retired soon after I came), mild-mannered until about 10 p.m. when he would become tipsy from his occasional trek out of the office. However, when he asked the sub-editors if they needed more copy, with a few phone calls, he would fill every crevice of the paper with stories gleaned from his telephone conversations.

There was Robert Best, Sunday Editor, (later Assistant Editor and then Editor), who was a gentle family man and there was Night Editor Ulric Rice, a man who rarely smiled and who could tell the dirtiest joke with his dead pan voice and a blank expression.

Tony Hinds was the beloved Librarian who could find a file of clippings on the devil, at the drop of the hat. Sports Editor O.S. Coppin cussed noisily, pants hitched up at regular intervals, as he, Clyde Walcott and Louis Brathwaite put the sports section to bed.

There was John Cumberbatch, who, on his return from university, became a teacher and a fierce trade unionist and there was Al Gilkes, who later made his name both as a columnist and by covering nerve-wracking stories and much later a public relations practitioner and an entertainment promoter. I remember, too, Paul Mandeville grey-eyed star photographer, who was as dedicated to football as he was to photography. Who could forget the messenger Reggie Haynes, who was the most revered member of staff as far as the public was concerned for he was one of the island's top and most loved and respected footballers.

Harold Hoyte, Fred Gollop and Carl Moore started The Nation newspaper in 1973.

There were the new-comers recently leaving school and cutting their teeth in journalism. Carl Moore, the tall, elegant, handsome sub-editor who spoke precisely and walked with a lopsided hop, characteristic of the legendary Sir Garfield Sobers. Carl, his shirt, always immaculate and opened half way down his chest, was to me as handsome and sexy as any film star. He eventually left *The Advocate*, joined *The Daily News*, then *Barbados Rediffusion* for a while, became the first Editor of *The Nation* and *Sunday Sun* newspapers and ended up being the Public Affairs Officer of the Central Bank of Barbados until his retirement.

Peter Simmons worked for a time as Director of Communications with the Barbados Government and ended up being Barbados's High Commissioner to London before his retirement from public life.

Then there was Harold Hoyte, a shy retiring sub-editor who was to blossom into the island's most celebrated journalist and co- founder then longest-serving founding Editor of *The Nation* newspaper.

There was Fred Gollop, co-founder of *The Nation* and, former President of the Senate, Chairman of One Caribbean Media, spanning media regionally. Sir Fred is also a director of First Caribbean CIBC Bank. There was Errol Humphrey, who became a trade technocrat and later Ambassador to Brussels.

There were two devilish but talented photographers, Gordon Brooks and Cyprian "Junior" LaTouche who, while driving me home, would go to a lovers' lane, fire his flash and startle the occupants "parked out" in cars. We never stayed around to see who they were.

Then there was me, Margaret Carter, who became the first female editor of a newspaper in The Bahamas, *The People*, and the first female and longest-serving Chief Information Officer of the Government Information Service of Barbados. Finally, there was Winston "Pop" Walker, an easy-going and constantly smiling sub-editor, who became Chief Sub-editor at *The Nation* until his retirement.

It was there at *The Advocate* that I learned that if you wanted to be treated as one of the boys, to gain their respect, you had to laugh at their jokes, share in their conversations, but always remain a lady. And never sleep with them. Laugh away the passes and move on to a serious subject.

It was a lesson that was to serve me in good stead as I worked with politicians and male civil servants. It was exposure which made me appear very worldly but in fact rather emotionally naïve. Because although there was nothing they didn't discuss with me, they treated me like a delicate possession. Daddy had told me stories of examples of this with Norton "Bimmy" Robinson, the most boisterous and irreverent of men on staff, and who would lift me, sleeping, cradled in his arms out of the van after a political meeting in some far-flung parish, and hand me to Daddy at the gate of my home.

Socially I did not lack for news for the social diary for even those who were not my friends or who were white would invite me to their parties to cover the events and then as a departure from *The Advocate*'s usual fare of focusing on big shots, I started covering working class events and putting their parties and birthdays and weddings in the paper.

I remember one incident with amusement. I went to Government House to cover a reception for a Heads of Government meeting and Ronald Mapp, Cabinet Minister, whom I called Uncle, for he was a close family friend, introduced me to Eric Gairy, Premier of Grenada. Minutes after I got home at about 10.30 p.m the phone rang and I answered and the person on the other end said: "This is Eric Gairy here. I am sending a car for you." I covered the phone with my hand and told my mother who took the phone from me and asked me to leave the room. She never told me what she said to him but he never called again.

December 1963 came and I said my goodbyes to this new world that I had enjoyed for the past two years and left by plane for London.

But why London? First, my best friend Angela Elder's boyfriend had gone to London with a number of young men to join the British Army and she was to follow and pursue secretarial studies.

Second, a group of young men who had been working in the West Indies Federal Government, when it broke up, came back to Barbados and were so mentally stimulating that I was drawn to them and loved listening to them argue and debate issues from politics to religion. I also enjoyed watching the foreign films which we showed at the Barbados Film Society which they had formed and of which I was an officer.

At one of those get-togethers I met Colin Hope, the man who was to become my husband. We dated for a month before he left for Paris where he had a job lined up with UNESCO. So London was the closest I could get to Paris and the chance of seeing Colin.

CHAPTER 6

LONDON

London was like a surrealist dream. I banished the beautiful liberty wool and silk suits Mummy had made for me, stopped straightening my hair and had a barber cut it into a short afro. I donned with my silk shirts a pair of red or black skin-fitting pants which I wore with red boots and large earrings. I was ready to take on London and leave Barbados behind.

But that was difficult. On Christmas day the snow fell—first snow for me; tiny flakes melting before they touched the earth. As I frolicked trying to catch them in my mouth, I was filled with the sound of my grandfather's voice describing snow to me and I longed for him.

Later, walking along the banks of the Thames, tears ran down my face as if trying to top up the levels of that beautiful murky river which English literature, like Dickens, had made live in the minds of colonial children like me and I was both glad of the anonymity yet longed to share the scenes with my grandfather and at the same time curl up in the bed with my mother and get warm.

I walked through parks at dusk and hummed to the forlorn crying of a bird high up in a tree, probably a nightingale. I stared at the snot nose black cabs but didn't dare to stop them. They seemed so unreal. And I wanted to hug every bobby I saw and would find excuses to talk to them.

I began a novel of a love affair between a young girl and an asexual man, dark sometimes, but warm with the passion girls who are fed on romantic literature like Jane Eyre, dreaming of finding and taming a Mr. Rochester. I had not yet read *The Sun Also Rises*, but was deeply involved with the character who found an echo in my own asexual nature.

There were a few harmless flirtations, with one young man in particular from Fiji, whom I knew, if I had ever kissed him, I would get a seizure. There was a St. Lucian who called me Makeba and who said with my short natural hairstyle I had become the third black woman in the western world to wear her hair like that, the others being the South African singer Miriam Makeba and Odetta, another famous singer.

My tight pants on my skinny body did very little for black men but many an evening an old or young white man, more often than not with a cough, would follow me from the station to my Earl's Court home and stand outside for a while before drifting off.

I grew tired of my kind northern England landlady's attempts to cook black food, curry with raisins and red lamb stew and fish stew, which an African boarder had taught her, so most evenings I would go to the West Indian Students Centre at No.1 Earl's Court to enjoy the food prepared by three rather large West Indian cooks who did their best to fatten me up with peas and rice and wicked stew washed down with a concoction of black current juice and something else which had a fancy name which I have forgotten.

Fred Gollop, my friend from *The Advocate*, and I ran for office at the Students Union as First Vice Presidents to President Fitzroy Bryant and Secretary Lee Moore, both law students like Fred. Fitzroy was a character but Lee was one of the most effete men I had ever known with a high-pitched voice, an English accent and a little dapper body and, as we say in the West Indies, a mob-a-ton of brains. He eventually became Prime Minister of St. Kitts/Nevis.

I became friends with a Jamaican, "handsome, articulate and black," as one English newspaper had described him when he was a spokesman for an organisation, the Campaign Against Racial Discrimination. Richard Small, the son of a judge, and I bonded like brother and sister and have remained friends for life. As was the case of his girlfriend, an exotic and beautiful half-

Ghanaian, half-Armenian young girl, Anoush, after whom my daughter was named. I was to make both of them my daughter's godparents many years later. Richard settled in Jamaica where he practised law and married twice.

I met a Ghanaian in London and started going out with him. An engineer, he was an official of the African Students Centre, a stone's throw away at No. 3 Earl's Court and I eventually assisted them with secretarial duties in an honorary position.

One unforgettable event happened there when I met Malcolm X who came to address the students. Kofi introduced me to African foods like foo foo, fried plantain cut like chips and red stews, tasting far superior to that offered by my landlady. He also took me to Ghanaian weddings, betrothals and christenings. Kofi and I remained lovers until I went home. He had told me once, when we were discussing marriage, that when I went to Ghana I would not be able to sit and hold discussions with men, I would have to sit with the women of the household or village. This ruled him out as a possible husband. He was a muscular, thick set, curly-haired black-skinned man who spoke softly. Love-making was comforting and relaxing and I was so relaxed that in February 1964 I stopped taking the Phenobarbitone and completely forgot I was epileptic.

I had a good friend, Gordon, who was a tall, bearded Guyanese with a sulky mouth. We didn't get close until he and his girlfriend broke up, leaving him totally shattered. He worked at the Students Centre and had more money than most students and would take me out to dinner to discuss his loss while smoking packs of cigarettes. To prevent myself from falling asleep, thus able to make soothing noises at the appropriate times, I would take a cigarette and thus began that bad habit which I only ended in 1984 after an intervention by my children.

Gordon had a Guyanese Indian friend, married to an Italian woman. They owned an Indian restaurant in Earl's Court which was very popular with the English theatre celebrities. We would dress nicely; the Liberty wool outfits which Mummy had made, came in handy, and go to dinner and were served with all the panache reserved for the rich and famous. After dinner, however, when the restaurant was empty of Peter O'Toole and Michael Caine and others, we would "sing for our supper" by folding napkins and laying tables.

My best friend Angela, who had come up to England and moved in with her brother, Rudy, and sister-in-law Jeannette, got married on July 10, 1965, to her soldier fiancé Cameron Knight and went to live in Germany. It was a pretty little wedding and I gave them an ice bucket shaped like a pineapple, which many years later when she was ill with Alzheimer's and didn't recognise me, still sat on her dining table. She died on November 6, 2010 – one of the saddest days of my life.

So passed my time in London, school, hectic parties, the poetry reading sessions at Cliff Lashley, a poet and librarian from Jamaica, who would take me to male gay parties, or domino sessions. Richard and Anoush would have a "do" and we would all go, the young and the not-so-young. And I remember one night dancing bare-footed to Nina Simone alone in the dim light surrounded by the others lounging on the carpet and John La Rose, a formidable Caribbean intellectual, penned a poem about me, published in his book of poems *Foundations*, which he called Margaret, Dancer.

> *Such delicacy of movement*
> *The fluttering fingers*
> *Feigned the drum*
> *Transported Africa*
> *Into her meaning*
>
> *Head*
> *Leg*
> *Torso and balled feet*
> *Intertwined in nuance;*
> *She wined*
> *Butterfly hands transposed*
> *Her enigma*
> *Punctilio*
> *Perched on her canvas*
> *Winging*
> *Winging beyond*

Then one evening the West Indian Students Centre was all abuzz. The great West Indian novelist Wilson Harris was coming to address us on West Indian literature and the even greater C.L.R. James was coming along. C.L.R. and his lovely wife Selma came and I met them and that was the beginning of a relationship which would last until his death, while mine and Selma's still exists.

CHAPTER 7

THE THIRD CONVULSION

Richard and I became very close to the Jameses and soon I was spending more time at their house than my own. Eventually, they invited me to come live with them at Staverton Road, Willesden Green, where I became the second child in the house, along with Selma's son, from her first marriage, 15-year-old Sam Weinstein, a quiet, amiable, thoughtful young man. I found the house warm with that careless lived-in feel and look. It had three bedrooms, a large living room partially lined with worn books and a small kitchen.

Margaret, standing, C.L.R. sitting; his wife Selma, left and stepson Sam, right.

Selma, who looked like a Jewish aristocrat with her shock of prematurely, slightly graying hair over high cheek bones and petite shapely body, was a working class girl who had met and loved C.L.R. during his American revolutionary period. She was about 35 and he was almost twice her age. She taught me so much; in fact, she and C.L.R. picked up my education where my grandfather had left off. He had made me read Tolstoy's *Anna Karenina*, but it was Selma who drew my attention to the importance of the first line in a novel in determining the quality of the book of which Anna was her best example. We listened to Chopin appreciatively and lesser musicians more critically. It was to give me a greater appreciation of classical music than that of our classical music classes at Foundation.

C.L.R. or "Nello", as she called him, was a tall, slim nut brown Trinidadian, who in his sixties was still handsome although his hands shook from when he was in his twenties. He spoke with a soft lilting voice and gestured like a conductor directing an orchestra while making a point.

A friend and a member of the C.L.R. James group, Norman Girvan, writing in 1988, described James as one of the most important persons of the 20th century. I quote his description of C.L.R. because in a few words it summed up his life.

He was describing his first encounter with James when James was 58. He wrote in a foreword to a book by a consortium of social scientists: "James had already lived three lives as a writer, literary critic and sportswriter in his native Trinidad in the 1920s; as sportswriter turned socialist and anti-imperialist writer and activist in Britain in the 1930s; as a Marxist and revolutionary scholar and organiser in the United States in the 1940s and 1950s. He was then in the midst of his fourth life as political writer and agitator in Trinidad as Secretary of the West Indies Federal Liberal Party and Editor of the *PNM organ*, *The Nation*, and later as founder of the Workers' and Farmers' Party."

Norman had gone on to describe his fifth life as teacher and mentor to several generations of Caribbean students and that is how we came into his life. Norman, a brown Jamaican graduate of the University of the West Indies was, now pursuing post graduate studies in economics.

The CLR Group was made up of the two Jamaican lawyers who had organised it Norman and lawyer Richard Small. (In 2014, at the height of Norman's intellectual life after years as a university professor, and one of the leading Caribbean intellectuals and activists, he died tragically while being treated in Cuba for injuries sustained from a fall from a cliff in Dominica while hiking with his family.)There was another Jamaican lawyer Adolph Edwards--a lawyer pursuing post graduate studies in law-. Then there were Selma James and Stanley French, engineer and playwright and St. Lucian; Wally Look Lai, a Trinidadian lawyer; Fennis Augustine, a Grenadian shop steward and me the would be poet and novelist.. But of the group the one who was to become the most famous of all, the physically small but formidable intellectual, and historian, Walter Rodney, whom I wish to comment on in some detail, although the period I speak of was way into the future.

I met Walter in the 60s in London, fresh from his studies at Mona Campus, UWI, along with members of the C.L.R. James Study Group – a band of passionate, young and committed persons. We respected and adored Walter and he became the unofficial spokesman of the group but we were also a little in awe of this fierce bearded young man who dared to challenge C.L.R. in debates on Marxism. On his return to the Caribbean he worked at the Mona campus, which he left at some time for a conference of Caribbean writers. He was refused entry back into Jamaica which led to popular riots in that country.

Years later in the 70s, after his sojourn in Africa and return to Guyana, he had to lecture in the United States to earn a living. In Guyana while his wife Pat pursued studies in Jamaica he, looked after his children, Shaka Kanini and Asha cooked pepper- pot for them and plaited his daughters' hair.

He was also busy organising politically, trying to forge unity between the African and Indian communities through the political organisation, the Working People's Alliance. When he came to Barbados to lecture at Cave Hill, the Barbados campus of the UWI, sometimes accompanied by one of his children, we would visit Worthing Beach. While our children played in the sand, he would share with me his dreams for Guyana—a racially united Guyana where all would have the chance to fulfill their promise without fear of intimidation or violence. And it was on one such occasion that he asked me to promise him that if anything happened to him, I should bring Pat and the children to Barbados. It was a promise I kept for something did happen to him.

Of all the things that Walter was and could have been to Guyana, the Caribbean and the world, the greatest tragedy is that he did not live to see the wonderful men and women that his children have grown into and to love his four grandchildren or see the powerful intellectual and matriarch that his beloved Pat, my close friend, has become as she works tirelessly to keep the flame he lit alive.

Walter's passing left a political and intellectual vacuum in the Caribbean and the world which has not yet been filled and probably never will. But I live in hope that his legacy will live on in our children and grandchildren that one day it will come to fruition.

We were sometimes joined by John Maxwell, a social worker, and once we were joined by Orlando Patterson, working on his first novel *Children of Sisyphus*, and who was to become one of the most celebrated of a new generation of West Indian novelists.

Selma was almost as important a mentor as C.L.R. and she encouraged our creative side. But when it wasn't Friday night with the regular group meeting, life fell into a routine. Selma worked in the day and came home and prepared dinner for Sam, C.L.R. and me which we usually ate sitting on the floor while C.L.R. stretched out on the sofa and spoke softly of the news, listened to music or watched TV and discussed a wide range of issues.

In the day, armed with Rita Springer's cookbook, I prepared C.L.R. West Indian dishes.

Let me digress. My mother used to give our cook the third Sunday off and my sister Diane–an 'A' student in domestic science at Queen's College–and I had to prepare lunch. I also did domestic science but struggled and my contribution to this lunch was laying the table, making the salad and mixing drinks, usually lemonade.

Amazingly, as if guided by some divine power, able only to prepare the basic recipe, the cup of cou cou and a small saucepan of salt fish butter sauce, (I didn't dare double the ingredients) it was often just enough for C.L.R.'s meal, which he said tasted like his mother's. It is surprising how lives get linked: Rita, the author of the cookbook, was the mother of the young man at whose party I had had my last convulsion.

While he ate stretched out on his bed or on the sofa with a tray, C.L.R. would make me read Proust and Sartre, Tolstoy and this and that to him. He would play Mozart and the Mighty Sparrow and point to the similarities in the musical phrasing. His world was magical and more strident than Selma's, but both were illuminating.

I have forgotten a lot of what I learned but in my conversations today with the Prime Minister of Barbados, Freundel Jerome Stuart, a well-read and powerful intellectual, he would make a point or posit a piece of philosophy and I would be transported back to those wintry evenings with Selma, Sam and C.L.R., sometimes joined by George Lamming and Richard Small.

I learned that Selma was going to Trinidad but before she left on August 7 she decided that they would have a 21st birthday party for me on August 6. Two things happened that built up tension in me. First, a young man whom I had known had had a convulsion in his bath tub and died the day before the party. Second, my mother was meeting Selma at the airport at Seawell in Barbados and I knew Mummy would ask about my health, particularly my epilepsy.

I had told nobody in England that I was epileptic and I knew my mother would question her relentlessly about my health.

The day of the party came. All of my friends were coming and I had a beautiful chiffon green dress to wear – which I had never worn – hoarding it as I was wont to do. Selma cooked up a storm and Sam and I, both excited, ran errands all day. We dressed. Selma in a black silk dress and Ethel Decaiser, George Lamming's girlfriend, who was head of the anti-apartheid movement in the United Kingdom and who had come early to help, also wore a black dress with a cowl neckline. Even George made an effort to be dapper.

To write this memoir I have consulted very little so except for the guests arriving, the remainder of the party passed like a dream. I don't even remember having an aura. I came to, stretched out in a settee between Selma and George, each of ny hands clasped by one of them. Crest-fallen, I was aware of what had happened and lay dazed hardly hearing or understanding their conversation in hushed tones in the dimly lit room.

The concerned look on my friends' faces made me feel so guilty. Richard stayed for a few days. If I dropped the soap in the bathroom, he or Kofi would be banging on the door fearing I had had another attack.

I fell apart. I was depressed and out of control. I slept all day and stayed awake all night. There was a constant mist of numbness which sunlight did not penetrate; I wanted my mother. I knew I couldn't cope any more and after a few months of drifting in the fog and hurting the people closest to me, Mummy sent for me.

I arrived in Barbados in the evening with my short afro and the next day my mother took me to a hairdresser to get my hair straightened.

In retrospect the most painful part of leaving London was ending my closeness with Selma. Except for the fire in her soul and her powerful intellect nothing I knew of her prepared me for the formidable woman she was to become and the shape her life was to take.

She today lives in a housing co-op with her partner Nina, who is also involved with the movement and the Global Women's Strike which is based at the Crossroads Centre.

The Crossroads Centre at 25 Wolsey Mews has been going on for over 40 years and is now much expanded and is involved with caring for and organizing with the rebellious and/or the dispossessed. Selma, who had become a prolific writer, had the anthology of her work published titled *Sex, Race and Class – the Perspective of Winning*. Recently, Crossroads Books published Ralph Ibbott's story of the Tanzanian socialist villages, *Ujamaa*, with a lengthy introduction by Selma and edited by her with assistance from Nina. Selma is one of the leading political women in the world and Wages for Housework has won international recognition if not total acceptance.

Sam married a Barbadian, Margaret Prescod, cousin of Barbados Prime Minister Freundel Stuart, is divorced and now lives in London with his love Lisa after a lifetime of work as a top official of the Utility Workers' Union of America (UWUA). He is also involved with the Crossroads Centre.

CHAPTER 8

MARRIAGE AND CHILDREN

Colin, with whom I had had a one-month non-sexual relationship when I was 18, had left for Paris to work with UNESCO and wrote me the most beautiful love letters for two years. He had come to London for a weekend within my first three months of being there. But nothing came of the relationship since on his return to Paris he wrote me a letter stating that a  relationship was not possible since he was involved with someone called Danielle and he would either destroy her or she destroy him.

Colin Chamberlain Macaulay Hope was a Barbadian whose father became Barbados's first King Scout and who was married to a Thorpe, an upper-class family member that had lawn tennis courts in their childhood in St. James. He was among the first students at the Mona campus of the University of the West Indies but didn't graduate. However, he went on to Toronto University in Canada where he graduated and then went to the University of Sweden where he got his master's. Years later, in the tenth year of our marriage, he earned a doctorate in political science from the University of the West Indies.

We drifted back together on my return to Barbados. This 5-foot 6-inch dapper man, 15 years my senior, had a face that to me was beautiful; so beautiful that when I first saw him I went home and told my mother: "Today I met a man that I want my children to look like."

We started dating seriously and a few months later he asked me to marry him and I accepted. In October 1966, a month before the independence of Barbados, we got married in the picturesque St. Andrew's Parish Church and spent our honeymoon at Edgewater Hotel in St. Joseph.

One of the readers of this book in manuscript thought that I should add this little postscript. The morning after the first night of my honeymoon my mother called me, the worldly Margaret, and in hushed tones, asked: "After last night, are you all right, darling?"

Colin was then employed in public relations at the Board of Tourism but applied for and received a job as Extra-Mural Tutor of the University of the West Indies, stationed in The Bahamas.

In January 1967, then a few months pregnant, we went to The Bahamas to New Providence and moved into the Tutor's house in Oaksfield. It was in a bad state of repair and after a few months Colin persuaded the university to renovate it, which they did. I was sent home to have the baby and he moved into an apartment.

I had a bad pregnancy, not being able to keep anything down and being hospitalised about three times. The orderlies got so used to seeing me that when I actually went into labour they made me walk up the stairs. And then the miracle happened: I gave birth to my beautiful five and a half pound baby daughter.

Achebe, Anoush, Margaret and Colin

I went home after a few days in hospital and Colin came for a few days. In September the renovations were complete and Anoush and I flew back to a spanking new home, beautifully furnished and outfitted.

At six months, Anoush caught a cold, her temperature shot up to 103 and she had her first convulsion. We panicked as she lay unconscious after the spasms subsided. But she recovered in a couple of hours and when the cold passed was her bubbly, lively self again. This was to repeat itself every time she had a high temperature. Her doctor, Herbie Husbands, who was married to my Ghanaian friend Anoush, the baby's godmother, assured us that childhood convulsions combined with a high temperature did not mean she was epileptic and we drew comfort from this information.

When she was two, she took in with an illness and Herbie said it could be polio and kept her in hospital for tests. Colin and I went home and crying, made love without contraception and 40 weeks later, after a good pregnancy, I went into labour which lasted two days and eventually a 10-pound baby boy was taken from me by caesarean section. But I had developed pneumonia and after I was discharged from hospital I was still too ill to breast feed Achebe.

I never forgot my birth control pills again but had no regrets for he was an absolute joy as a little boy and grew into a tall, handsome, charming – sometimes too charming – young man.

I wrote a poem about him watching him one day when he had brought home two of his little children and Anoush's daughter from a day out. He supervised their baths and then sat on a bar stool as they consumed Kentucky fried chicken dinners.

> *Achebe*
> *To see your face soften*
> *As you smile with children*
> *Is to see the wide-eyed boy I knew*
> *Before life robbed him of his innocence and left its mark*
> *To see the trust*
> *The love*
> *The flutter of masculine softness*
> *You now shield from sight of all*
> *But children*

I started working as a freelance writer and then as an on-staff reporter and then as News Editor of *The Bahamian Times*, the governing party's newspaper. This closed and I was appointed Editor of *The People*, a newspaper mainly focused on selling the idea of independence to the people of The Bahamas.

The Bahamas is made up of 700 islands, about 13 being habitable, and we lived in the capital, New Providence. Boasting some of the most spectacular beaches in the Caribbean, New Providence was not a particularly attractive island, covered as it was by pine trees with their forlorn fronds like scarecrows reaching for the sky. The Bahamian people were very friendly but much Americanised and very different from the people of the rest of the Caribbean of whom they did not consider themselves a part.

The family islands, as the other islands were called, also featured spectacular beaches and when we lived there in the late 60s and early 70s were very underdeveloped. Our lives in The Bahamas were very exciting. We had busy social lives, made many friends and remain in contact with several.

Four I wish to mention: socialite, Esther Culmer, mother of three and married and divorced from a Bahamian doctor, Kirk; Betty Nixon, my beloved secretary, married to Oswald Nixon and parents of many children, Beryl Hanna, English wife of the Deputy Prime Minister at the time, later to become Governor–General, Sir Arthur Hanna and Jamaican journalist Sonia Mills, a part Chinese mother of two and married to Don Mills a career civil servant and diplomat..

In 1972 Colin was transferred to Grenada as Extra-Mural Tutor and I packed up the children and went back to Barbados where my mother was living or rather dying from breast cancer. Anoush was five at the time and had stopped having the temperature-related seizures. Achebe was as healthy as a horse but did not speak until his second birthday.

I joined the Government Information Service in 1972, where I met and became firm friends with my boss Gladstone Holder, an eccentric, tall, broad-chested man, with a strange haircut which attracted the nickname of "Muff" by the school boys he taught before joining GIS. Muff wore pants, especially tailored with wide "sailor" bottoms.

He was an avid reader and loved to discuss literature, history, politics and whatever subjects young members of staff like Peter Greene, Arthur Morris and I challenged him to engage in.

My mother, after many blood transfusions, died in June of 1973, leaving me bereft. Colin completed his assignment and returned to Barbados where he joined the staff of the Erdiston Teachers' College in the same compound where Anoush and Achebe were in elementary school and nursery school, respectively.

After my mother's death I felt an urgent need to be left alone and grew confused as our marital problems persisted when all I wanted to do was sleep and be left to myself. We sought counselling with psychiatrist Dr. George Mahy. George suggested that for a while Colin should move into another room but he wouldn't budge and eventually I took the children and left him.

In 1976 I was seconded to the Caricom Secretariat as a UNESCO media consultant on the Regional Food Plan in Georgetown, Guyana. I enjoyed the freedom and being in the country where my mother had grown up and which happened also to be the friendliest place I had ever lived. Near the end of the first six months of my one-year secondment, Anoush had a convulsion at elementary school which was not associated with a temperature. I asked that I be allowed to serve out my last six months in Barbados and was given an office at the Cave Hill campus of the University of the West Indies.

Anoush continued to have seizures at school and Dr. Bertie Graham said she was now clearly epileptic. She suffered torment at the hands of the children at school. I remember going to a beach party and she was helping our hostess serve cake and one child, who was at Erdiston with her, told her: "I don't want cake from a nasty girl." I left the party but I hurt with pain for her and guilt from the belief that if I had not left Barbados she would not have gotten ill.

My marriage ended but the children were not deprived of their father since he came and did homework with them almost every day and often had Sunday lunch with us. We finally divorced in 1978. (Colin was a very nurturing and loving father. So grateful was I for that that when he became ill, with an infected heart valve, I took him into my home, where he resided until his death in December 2012.)

Around this time the struggle of looking after the children, working hard and long hours, for I was now a senior at GIS in charge of the Press Section, a rape by an 18- year-old resulted in a bout of depression for which I had to be hospitalised. I remained at the hospital for about two weeks.

The rape occurred in the bedroom, bathed by the glow of a tall street lamp, in the house "Brumaran", where I had lived in Sergeant's Village and where I had returned in 1978, now a single mother.

I was in my house with the two children asleep in their rooms at the top of the stairs and down from the master bedroom, which is in the front of the house and running the width of the house. I had jumped out of my sleep awakened by the creaking of the old staircase. I ran to the top of the stairs where I saw a man with a knife in his hand coming up the stairs. I took a plant pot that decorated the top of the stairs, and threw it at him and he ran back down the stairs.

Three nights later I was awakened again by a man lying on me pulling up my night gown and with a knife at my throat. I could see his face from the street light which flooded the room and all I kept repeating as he raped me was: "Did you hurt my children; are my children all right?" When it was soon over – briefly, thank God – he patted my head with the hand holding the knife and said something, which I don't remember. He left me and climbed back through the upstairs window on to the roof and must have jumped down for I did not wait to see but rushed to check on my children, who were both sleeping soundly.

I don't remember if I called Colin first and he called the Police or if I called the Police and then called him, but soon they were both there and thus began the cross-examination. Was I wearing panties? and so on.

The next day a female police officer and Colin took me to a doctor for an injection against sexually-transmitted disease. For weeks I would receive phone calls from policemen asking if I was wearing panties. Or two would come up in a car, get out and patrol in front of the house and throw pebbles at the window and when I went to it they would ask me if I had on panties. One of them, a good-looking gentle policeman became my stabilising force and he told me that one of a set of kitchen knives from my kitchen was found in the house of an old woman up the road who had been raped by two men. I had described the man as light brown with a very big nose. I pointed out that I too had a big nose and was used to big noses, so when I said that he had a big nose I meant it was very big. Apparently they raped a pregnant white girl who gave a similar description. The involvement with the police continued until they invited me to an identification parade where I identified my rapist. And I was told he was 18 years old, a few years older than my daughter.

A year passed and the case was called before Justice Lindsay Worrell. Half way through the hearing the young man dismissed his lawyer and in so doing got so agitated when he was charged with breaking into my house, he said he did not have to break in; he could open the windows from the outside, thus placing himself at the scene of the crime. The case ended with him getting 10 years in jail and 10 lashes with the cat-o-nine-tails. I, who had survived the year, left the court crying and went to George Mahy's office still crying for myself, the victim, and for the 18-year-old perpetrator who had said in his defence that he used drugs and when he came home late his mother never let him in. Then he would get on his bicycle and ride all over Barbados until morning.

I told George I could not cope anymore. He directed that I be admitted to the Queen Elizabeth Hospital, where I spent a few days. That was 1979. It left me with an urgent need to get out of my beloved "Brumaran" and to live somewhere where the houses were so close that if you sneezed the neighbours would hear it, hence, the purchase of my current home, surrounded by houses close by.

Despite the move to the new house for many years I would hear footsteps and lie paralysed in my bed until I had the courage to get up and turn on the light to satisfy myself there was no one there. I still lock my bedroom door at night.

The period from 1978 to 1986 was fraught with the tensions of making ends meet and trying to maintain the world to which my children had grown accustomed but were beginning to reject as a meaningless, sterile, cruel place. They still went to the middle-class parties but their choice of close bosom friends was the more human, less prejudiced, working-class children who had joined them in university or in social groups dedicated to helping the underprivileged, particularly in Anoush's case, children with disabilities, or in Achebe's, sports clubs.

Let me say something about my rise up the ladder at GIS. I joined as Assistant Information Officer on December 1, 1972, coming from being newspaper editor in the Commonwealth Bahamas and was appointed in February, 1973, and was assigned, as an experiment, as Public Relations Officer stationed in the Ministry of Trade.

It was at this time that I conceived Consumer Diary, a list of basic food items, recipes and comparison of prices for radio, television and press. In

1975 1 was promoted to Information Officer and worked in the TV section producing videos and TV programmes and supervising the officers.

Later I was promoted to Senior Information Officer responsible for implementing a full public relations system. In May 1982, I was appointed to the newly-created position of Deputy Chief Information Officer during the trying time of the Grenada coup and the perception that the whole region was in turmoil. During a two-year stint at the Board of Tourism I organised Barbados's participation at an Expo in Vancouver, Canada, and hosted with attorney Jack Dear, a dinner for a hundred of the much-maligned beach vendors at the Hilton Hotel.

I returned to GIS in 1985. One of my achievements of which I am proudest is the publication arm with Samantha Jones which flourished with the encouragement of the four Ministers of Information: Sir Lloyd Sandiford, the Rt. Hon. Owen Arthur and the two other Ministers of Information at other times, Sir David Simmons and the Hon. Mia Mottley, producing technical and academic publications with papers by public officers, outstanding speeches by ministers and coffee-table books. Another outstanding achievement was the GIS campaign for the introduction off VAT and an AIDS campaign.

Before becoming Chief I had directed and produced with cinematographer Peter Roy Byer the story of the first free village in Barbados at Rock Hall, featuring my friend, the then Professor Woodville Marshall, later Sir Woodville, and historian Ronnie Hughes, and narrated by George Lamming. We faced many obstacles as we tried to finish the 45-minute documentary until Prime Minister Tom Adams intervened and ordered that until it was finished Roy and I were to work on nothing else. He was so proud of the film that he orchestrated a premiere in Rock Hall, the village in his constituency of St. Thomas, to which he invited President of Zambia, Kenneth Kaunda, who had spent a night in Barbados.

Tom Adams was a strange man who was liked and hated with equal intensity. He was self-confident, with a wry sense of humour, had an absolutely remarkable memory and was almost childishly overwhelmed by loyalty.

Two examples of these characteristics will suffice. At lunch at Government Headquarters one day he joined my table and after social chit chat produced a letter I had written to him in the early sixties inviting him to join the Film Society and recommending that he come to see an op art film, "The Cranes Are Flying". Like an elephant he never forgot.

His self–confidence and sense of humour were evidenced at the Hilton Hotel when United States President Ronald Reagan was visiting Barbados. He was about to enter a room where a press conference with the two leaders was to be held. The Prime Minister bent to comb his hair in the reflection of my always-foggy glasses and said: "Hopey, if you saw me and the President and you didn't know who was who, which one would you say was President of the United States?"

Tom Adams died at 52 in 1985 and was succeeded by the person I considered the most honest and decent politician that I had worked with, Sir Harold St. John, and whom I had adored from my "girlhood". With my grandfather we used to join him as he chatted with fishermen in Oistins, clad in a little white shirt and white shorts, his curly hair in knots.

He too called me "Hopey" and called me often at the Board of Tourism or on my return to GIS as Chief to find out "what is going on". A few months later, in 1986, when he lost the government and his seat, I cried all night and got up early next day to go to Government House for the swearing-in of Errol Barrow as Prime Minister. During the press conference Mr. Barrow turned to me and said: "You were crying all night for your boy; you should have worn dark glasses."

Mr. Barrow had served as Premier and then as Prime Minister for 15 years, from 1961 to 1976, the first five years as Premier. He became Prime Minister again in 1986 for a year and after his death in 1987, he was succeeded by a personal friend and one of my ex-husband's closest friends, Erskine Sandiford. Later Sir Lloyd, he was a Barbados scholar and student of governance, his great legacy was taking Barbados through a very bad economic crisis which left the island and the exchange rate intact. After his defeat in a no-confidence motion after which he called the elections he was defeated and succeeded by small dapper Owen Arthur, a bright economist who was still in office when I retired as Chief of GIS in 2003.

The author with then Prime Minister of Barbados Sir Lloyd Sandiford (centre) and then Vice President of the USA Mr. Dan Quayle.

In an interview with Carol Martindale of *The Nation* and Heather Greenidge of *The Advocate* on my retirement I commented on the Prime Ministers I worked with: "They were all bright; all loved pens and books," and I added, "It almost seems that to be Prime Minister those are the three criteria as well as being shy." I noted that Adams and Sandiford had similar prime ministerial styles, while Barrow and Arthur were more down-to-earth. I noted that St. John was of a different mould but had a better grasp than the others of the areas for which he had responsibility.

I need to explain why I mention the Prime Ministers in my memoir. I had worked closely with all five up to the Hon. David Thompson and Rt. Hon. Freundel Stuart and I hardly think that there are three public officers, alive or dead, who would have worked in such a sensitive post with all the Prime Ministers as Deputy or as Chief Information Officer.

Indeed, when I retired in 2003 and the newspaper published my interviews, Sir Lloyd, Sir Harold and the incumbent, Owen Arthur, called to wish me the best, thanking me for my service to their governments and to them and were pleased that I had served and had left without recrimination, bitterness or regret. Advising the Government and the Prime Minister on information was the number one job of the Chief Information Officer

I received the Silver Crown of Merit (SCM) for meritorious service to mass communications, in particular as an officer of the Government Information Service in 2011 from Governor General, His Excellency Sir Elliott Belgrave. The years at GIS – 29 on the payroll – were exciting and creative. I travelled with the Prime Ministers sending back reports to the local newspapers. We conducted the press affairs of visits of Queen Elizabeth II, President Clinton and Presidents from Venezuela, and Heads of State from Ghana, Zambia, Nigeria, Lesotho and Tanzania. My staff and I supervised the press at the State Opening of Parliament and officiated at national awards ceremonies at Government House.

The author receiving the Silver Crown of Merit (SCM) from Governor General, His Excellency Sir Elliott Belgrave.

In 1987, I had another depression. This period was very stressful. The staff had grown hostile to directives and decisions coming from the then Minister of Information. I was not sleeping well and was waking up after an hour or two with my tongue bitten up. I was hospitalised and psychiatrist George Mahy introduced phenobarbitone into my treatment and I can clearly remember the world righting itself about two hours after the dosage. I have not had another psychological break since that day.

Despite the stress of the job during the last two years of my working life, I completely enjoyed GIS and had an excellent relationship with the staff.

Arthur Morris, an officer of the early years, described me in a poem entitled "Hope":

> *Welcoming, exuberant, caring,*
> *That is her way with people.*
> *Thoughtful, intelligent, understanding.*
> *That was her style at work.*
> *Her heart is more gold than most*
> *She'll give you her last penny*
> *Whether it would help or not.*
> *Comfortable in her own skin, some might say*
> *Who is perfect? MCH is simply iconic*
> *With the flair for the dramatic.*
> *This perfectly good woman represents*
> *The best of the women of Barbados.*

In January 1996, concerned that although I was on the Phenobarbitone I had started waking again with my tongue bitten up, suggesting that I was having seizures in my sleep, I had been grappling with the children, now teenagers and demanding more time and more freedom, Achebe started to spend the week at Colin and when he came home he was testy.

More money was needed and thanks to kind bank managers I did not collapse, although things were hard. In 1996 I went to neurologist Dr. Sean Marquez who indicated that I was active again and put me on a dose of Tegretol and the sore tongue eventually went away. I was on the Tegretol until June 2004 when he started to reduce the dosage and by December I was completely off that medication. He continues to monitor me every six months but I have had no auras or bitten tongue or depressions since.

I retired in 2003 the day before my 60th birthday, and the sentiments expressed by the younger generation that I had worked with, established the mother role that I had assumed as I trained them for succession. The last two stanzas of the poem they included in a photo album of my farewell function read:

Will we still be your children?
Now you no longer need borrow a pen
Though you never know if you just might
But if so, would you pass by again
Can you still smile when you see us?
Just to remind us that all this time
Somehow we made your life happy
And that we will always remain in your mind
Will we still be your children?
Long after you depart
Will you still know how much you're missed?
Deep inside our hearts
Will you still be that one rock?
On which we could always depend
When the door has been closed and the goodbyes said
Can we still be your children?

And they certainly were, for in January 2004 I received an appointment as Chief Executive Officer of the Arnott Cato Foundation, a charity targeted at human resource development at the Queen Elizabeth Hospital, a job I enjoyed and held for 10 years until my retirement in June 2014. This job would have been impossible without the phone calls to "my children" at GIS on how to move a paragraph or something equally substantial as I became chief, secretary, clerk and accountant as I carried out the job from home alone, without the support of secretarial and administrative staff that I had for the 31 years at GIS. I was also grateful for the support of the Board, especially Chairman Sir Carlisle Burton and his successor Sir Errol "Mickey" Walrond.

Top left to right, Ayden, Jasmine,
Bottom left to right, Jayden, Isabella, Kemal and Nathan

That is my story; the story of an epileptic or a person with epilepsy, whichever you choose.

The drama of my life has left me grateful for the quiet, uneventful days and nights, now that I am fully retired. I spend my hours of retirement keeping in touch with old friends at home and abroad, visiting my children and grandchildren and loving them: Kemal (unofficially adopted), Jasmine, Jayden, Aydan, Isabella and the baby Nathan. I will continue to spend time in Germany, where my daughter lives with her German husband and child, and in the United States where my son lives. I will continue to entertain and love my nieces and nephews: Frantz, Gaea, Danielle and Dominic.

You may well ask what happed to Diane, Bruce and Woodie. Diane worked as a banker and became part of management before marrying Brian Griffith and giving birth to one child, Frantz and becoming a housewife.

Dominic, Danielle, Frantz, Anoush, Gaea and Achebe

Bruce, who became a lawyer after a few years of private practice, joined the public service and has worked as Principal Crown Counsel, Chief Legal Officer and ended his career as Commissioner of Titles. He was married to Jem Jeffers, a close friend of mine, and later to Barbara Tatem. He and Gem had one child Danielle.

Woodie, who was also a lawyer, ended a lengthy public service career at the top of the legal public service as Solicitor General of Barbados. He has two children, Gaea and Dominic.

.I am reasonably comfortable; financially more so because of the knowledge that my children will not let me suffer. I pass my time alone in my comfortable home feeding my mind with books, with television, with writing, with discussions on the telephone and with loving the characters who populated my life: politicians and work colleagues, family, friends, school friends with whom I get together occasionally, comrades living and dead and by forgiving those who had hurt me, out of innocence, ignorance or jealousy, comforted by the fact that I am truly a contented woman.

If I have seemed to have rambled through my story, I beg you to forgive me but my brain works in fits and starts, remembering some things with fierce clarity and forgetting people and places, and books and films as if they never were. Indeed, I just remembered, as I bring this tale to an end that one of the remarkable events in my life was my meeting with the late great South African leader Nelson Mandela when I joined a former Prime Minister of Barbados Sir Lloyd Sandiford at breakfast with him in Washington. I don't blame everything on my epilepsy but it has never let its grip on me go.

Bruce, Margaret, Diane and Woodie liming at Crystal Waters Hotel.

My relationship with epilepsy continues for my daughter Anoush is still an active epileptic but let her tell her own story. Before she does, let me tell you what she means to me.

> My Anoush
> My joy
> My comforter
> My friend
> A daughter and much more
> You who have enveloped me with love
> Which keeps me sane?
> In this insane world
> Where love is bargained
> As a price for freedom
> You who offer it freely
> God's child
> And mine.

CHAPTER 9

ANOUSH'S TALE

Anoush Hope-Fischer was born and grew up on the island of Barbados. Yesterday Was a Woman was her first novel and she received a Special Prize of Commendation from the Frank Collymore Literary Endowment of Barbados at the 10th anniversary awards in 2008. She holds a BA in Sociology and History and an MA in Special Education. She is a university lecturer in Germany, where she lives with her German husband and daughter.

In *Tested* I attempted to present my 'Situation and story' (Vivian Gornick) with as much objectivity as writing about a challenging and sometimes painful personal experiences will allow. And I have tried as much as possible to cut out the whining, complaining, sentiments of resentment and self-justification that often accompany reflection on experiences we don't want to face. Finally, I have tried to be creative in sharing these experiences without being an absolute bore.

My aim is to present this life-long experience to help families, caregivers, teachers, friends, co-workers, neighbours and the wider community to understand and appreciate the challenges that persons living with epilepsy face as they struggle through childhood and adolescence, learn to love and strive for independence and self-determination in adulthood.

More importantly, I write this for young people everywhere who struggle with this disease, that they may know that they are not alone in their experiences and so that they may have hope for a brighter tomorrow.

To live with epilepsy is to co-exist with something lurking in the shadows. In fact, it is only the daily preventative "pill popping" that serves as a reminder that something is physically out of sorts inside my body. I live with the eternal hope that I will one day be miraculously cured so I am still taken by surprise whenever I find myself lying flat on my back.

I try to liken the experience of epilepsy to other illnesses like asthma or hypoglycaemia. But with these chronic diseases there are clear warning signals that the body is heading towards a crisis. With epilepsy, it's more like an ambush or the attack of a ferocious beast.

WHAM! Without warning, it throws me down hard even before I know what has hit me. A body slam and I'm thrown on my back or on my side or on my face.

And for this reason I have likened it to a stalking predator on the attack. Very softly it follows my every move, waiting patiently for the right moment to strike, which I have to say is often quite inconvenient. And then, when I am hopeful that he might leave me be, suddenly launching a full attack, giving me no time to protect myself or flee.

ATTACK IN PARADISE

It is possible that when one thinks of paradise what comes to mind is brilliant warm sunshine, the shimmering blue ocean, coconut palms and beautiful scantily- clothed natives strolling along the golden sand of a lonesome beach. Someone else dreaming of paradise may imagine a lush jungle of exotic flowers with wild creatures prowling through the dense brush. Not omitting, of course, those beautiful scantly- clothed natives swimming in pools beneath roaring waterfalls.

The Caribbean region can throw at you any one or more of these combinations and, compared to many other parts of the world, is truly paradise. But the Caribbean is so much more. It's also the daily grind of not-so-beautiful bodies rushing to and from work, taking out the trash, throwing together a meal, washing the dishes and putting tuckered out grouchy children to bed. It is the scorching sun that makes bodies sweat and run for shelter. It is not so sunny days with powerful storms throwing crashing waves against the beach and lashing homes with whipping rain.

Wake up reader, the Caribbean is also like the rest of the world. And it is in this real Caribbean, this enigma of experiences, that I grew up. My paradise is a tiny island called Barbados. Northeast of Venezuela, set-slightly apart from the Windward Island chain, out in the wild raging Atlantic Ocean.

And paradise it certainly is with coconut trees, sunshine "fuh days" and beautiful people doing what people do every day. But it is so much more. It is a politically stable country which sits high up on the human development index, the economic index and the quality of life index. So life is sweet in Barbados.

It is on this "sweet fuh days" island that I experienced myself as a daughter, a sister, a niece, a friend, a lover and a co-worker. But my experience extends to that which less than one percent of all the citizens on my island paradise have ever had. With no jungle or plains in sight on this flat coral gem, I have been attacked by a beast unlike any other prowling this earth.

And during this violation, I can no longer feel the warm sunshine on my skin, see the swaying coconut trees, smell the raw ocean or hear the crashing waves.

I cannot appreciate or admire the beautiful or not-so-beautiful bodies passing by. And luckily for me I am not witness to the expressions of terror and shock on the faces of frightened children and bewildered adults who are unfortunate enough to be standing nearby. I believe it is a blessing that I cannot register their despair for how many islanders have ever seen such an attack.

I have epilepsy.

It would be great to say *had* epilepsy, but then, maybe, I would not have had the motivation to set the words on the page.

On these pages I throw open my life with the hope that somewhere a reader may extract some hidden truth that enriches their own and of those they love.

Away with you, beast of prey. Leave me be.

Paradise is not paradise for all who live here. As you will soon see.

GOOD MORNING, MISS EPILEPTIC

For a long time I thought of myself as epileptic. You know, like a title: "Good morning, Miss Epileptic! How you feeling, Miss Epileptic? Ain't you the one dat does get fits? Better lie down and take it easy. Miss Fits."

It took a long time before I stopped using those words "epileptic" and "fits". It took a long time before I thought of myself as a person with epilepsy – which meant I was more – a mother, a wife, a daughter, a sister, a lover, a friend, a colleague and a graduate of two universities with BA and MA degrees.

So what is this thing called epilepsy and what does it feel like?

The beast is on the prowl and I am the prey. I sense its approach on the surface of my skin. The tingling in my feet, a warning he is not so far away. I see him as he slinks by in my head, shooting glances that pierce my skull.

Then he strikes, attacking me. This powerful beast grabs hold where it can and shakes me until my teeth and bones are rattling. I fall, hitting my head, my face, and my arms on any surface nearby. He's holding me and shaking me still, so I throw my arms this way and that in an effort to fight him off. I try to curl my legs around him but it is not possible to trap him. He is too quick. I cry for help but no one hears for only a strange and gurgling sound escapes my lips.

I have no control. Even with guns, spears and medication. I can't fight off this beast. I just have to face him and hope for the best. The beast does not devour me; he loses interest and lets me go. Finally I am free of him but dead to the world.

This is the last time I think to myself and like a cat with nine lives, I am resurrected again.

Many people with epilepsy aren't aware of the warning signals of an attack. So I consider myself one of the lucky ones. I hear the beast roaring in my head, the rustle of the grass, the smell of his skin and the smell of his breath as he draws near. I know when it is going to happen and although I am filled with fear, I have a chance to alert those around me, save myself if possible, knowing that whatever I happen to be doing at that moment – standing on stage, taking an examination or liming with friends – the event is postponed until further notice.

Unfortunately an epileptic seizure happens not only to me but affects everyone nearby at the time. My mother, my father, my brother, teachers, friends, beautiful, or not-so-beautiful bodies on the beach, the rastas in Temple Yard and most unfortunately, the boyfriend I was kissing, are there to see what happens when this horrible creature jumps on my back.

How frightening it must be to witness an attack and be unable to do anything about it. My audience can't do much else but wait until the beast loses interest and lets me go and I am resurrected.

A NEW LIFE

I was born in 1967 and at the age of 48 I have had my share of experiences. My earliest experiences with epilepsy were told to me. My dad, who developed a quirky lifelong habit of placing the back of his hand on my forehead and neck, reported that every time I had a fever as an infant I had a seizure. It seemed to me a tall tale whenever he said it and as a mother myself I have learnt that fever is a normal part of the development of the immune system. But there was little talk of immune system at that time and even less chance for a fever to be a good thing so I caused my parents much worry.

By the time I was eight, I was having seizures often enough to have to be medicated and the spillover effects leave a sour taste in my mouth. I suffered, probably not as terribly as other children with the same illness. Much of the day I felt like I was walking around in a fog. It was difficult to concentrate in school and I had very little appetite. Returning to my primary school for a visit many years later, a teacher told me that she would always bring food back to the class after lunch and make me eat it. But it certainly was not fun and preparing for and writing exams was pure hell.

My teen years were somewhat better. I took the medication sporadically and, under the directive of a friend, cared somewhat less (but not less enough) about what other people thought. Still, it was not easy and I walked around with the constant fear that the beast would attack and expose me for all to see. I struggled through teen life juggling raging hormones, issues of self-worth, those first heartaches and the trials and tribulation of passing exams and getting through school. On top of it all I had to keep the beast at bay.

By the time I was seventeen my life was in turmoil and I was steeped in self-pity. My mother became ill for two weeks and no one would tell me what was wrong or what to do about it, although I realised later that it was probably epileptic-induced depression for she too was epileptic. I had made it out of school just barely and looking back now I was depressed. I searched high and looked outside myself for all the questions that torment young people in crisis.

The best advice I received was given to me by my father, who told me to do something worthwhile for someone else so I would be forced to pay less attention to myself.

And this led to an awakening.

So I joined a voluntary organisation which supported families with children with moderate to severe disabilities. Started by the National Children's Home, a British NGO, the organisation consisted mainly of mothers from low-income families. The group sought to influence government to provide support and services for all children with disabilities and support each other. An extension of this organisation was a group of young people who voluntarily provided respite for parents during the summer holidays and I joined the youth group in my quest to find fulfillment.

We received intensive training and in spite of the hard work and sleepless nights, I had a wonderful carefree summer with lots of fun and no time to focus on my own woes.

The year that followed I turned myself outward. I was in such a good space that I did not feel embarrassed or worried about my seizures. I had found home and I came to the realisation that there were happy people carrying greater burdens than my own.

The following summer I participated in a pre-camp seminar which changed my perception of myself. The trainer was an Englishman who brought video tapes to highlight different types of disabilities, appropriate ways of dealing with children with special needs and appropriate emergency responses.

One of those video tapes was on epilepsy and showed various children and adults having seizures. I sat in the session as if carved from stone. It was the first time I had ever seen what that beast did to me. I walked out of the session and found myself crouched under a huge tree, tears rolling down my face.

The trainer was annoyed that I had abruptly walked out of the class but the images were too much for me to handle. Eventually the session ended and someone wandered over and asked what was wrong.

But I could not speak. It was not possible to explain that I had suddenly realised that because of that terrible beast, I too was a person with special needs.

PLEASE GOD, SEND A CURE

Mark (9:14-29, the Message)

14-16 When they came back down the mountain to the other disciples, they saw a huge crowd around them, and the religion scholars cross-examining them. As soon as the people in the crowd saw Jesus, admiring excitement stirred them. They ran and greeted him. He asked, "What's going on? What's all the commotion?"

17-18 A man out of the crowd answered, "Teacher, I brought my mute son, made speechless by a demon, to you. Whenever it seizes him, it throws him to the ground. He foams at the mouth, grinds his teeth, and goes stiff as a board. I told your disciples, hoping they could deliver him, but they couldn't."

19-20 Jesus said, "What a generation! No sense of God! How many times do I have to go over these things? How much longer do I have to put up with this? Bring the boy here." They brought him. When the demon saw Jesus, it threw the boy into a seizure, causing him to writhe on the ground and foam at the mouth.

21-22 He asked the boy's father, "How long has this been going on?"

"Ever since he was a little boy. Many times it pitches him into fire or the river to do away with him. If you can do anything, do it. Have a heart and help us!"

23 Jesus said, "If? There are no 'ifs' among believers. Anything can happen."

24 No sooner were the words out of his mouth than the father cried, "Then I believe. Help me with my doubts!"

25-27 Seeing that the crowd was forming fast, Jesus gave the vile spirit its marching orders: "Dumb and deaf spirit, I command you—Out of him, and stay out!" Screaming, and with much thrashing about, it left. The boy was pale as a corpse, so people started saying, "He's dead." But Jesus, taking his hand, raised him. The boy stood up.

As a teen, I used to hound my neurologist down for a cure. One day, as I sat before him, tears streaming down my face, it was probably out of frustration that he said:

"Don't worry too much about it my dear, most people grow out of them and by the time you are an adult the seizures will have stopped."

What a relief that was at the time and what a load of crock. I am soon fifty and still waiting for the attacks to stop. I am still waiting for the cure.

It is estimated that 1 in 100 persons will have epilepsy or experience a seizure. The idea that epilepsy is a supernatural, demonic or spiritual disorder persisted along with widespread beliefs that it was due to possession by the devil. This notion of supernatural possession is supported from the miracle story of the cure of the epileptic child recorded in the Gospels.

Epilepsy was also viewed as a result of a person perpetrating evil doings, or as a consequence of cycles of the moon or mystic phenomena. In Roman times, people with epilepsy were given a special stone to smell. If they did not fall to the ground on smelling the stone, they were considered free of the "falling sickness." (This was a common procedure when buying slaves.)

Many treatments were experimented with in attempts to treat the illness through the medical Dark Ages. Plants like mistletoe and valerian plus spells, crystals, seeds and stones were used. Later, metals like copper and zinc and even mercury were also given to patients and blood-letting or skull trephination was performed.

It was only in the 19th and 20th centuries that rational and scientific notions and medicines replaced the primitive concepts and truly helpful medicines were discovered and tried. The first of these was potassium bromide, introduced in 1857 by obstetrician Sir Charles Locock. At the time, bromide was used as a sedative and was known to have anti-aphrodisiac qualities. (Thank God I was not born at that time!)

Epilepsy was believed to result from sexual excitement. Locock decided to test bromides in the treatment of seizures and the treatment proved effective BUT the side effects were debilitating and included drowsiness, fatigue, nausea, vomiting, acne, skin rash, blurred vision, dizziness, mania, hallucinations, increased thirst, hunger and urination, pancreatitis, muscle weakness, hypothyroidism, poor memory, psychosis, coma, possible attention deficit hyperactivity disorder (ADD/ADHD) in children and loss of sex drive.

And although it was known by the 1950s that it was not the suitable choice of treatment, bromides were still available for treatment in some countries in the 1970s and are used today for treating pets with epilepsy.

The first major breakthrough in epilepsy therapy came in 1912, with release of the barbiturate Phenobarbital by German company Bayer & Co. Phenobarbital was originally used as a sedative and hypnotic, and its anti-convulsant properties were stumbled upon by Alfred Hauptmann, a young physician, who used the drug to sedate his epileptic patients.

The drug continues to play a significant role in the treatment of epilepsy and is recommended by the World Health Organisation as first-line treatment for tonic-clonic seizures (partial and general) in the developing world. But again the side effects of dizziness, drowsiness, clumsiness or unsteadiness seem daunting.

I am not certain about the bromides but I am certain during my late primary school years and early teens I was prescribed Phenobarbital. I cannot remember the dizziness although there were several instances as a child where I found myself paralysed by fear of heights and had to be rescued. But I do remember the drowsiness and clumsiness. The drowsiness affected my performance in school. But one painful incident happened when I was ten and spending time with a family. While helping quite proudly to set the table, I kept banging the dishes. A family member flew into a rage, cursing me and calling me names including a clumsy idiot. It was such a painful experience that for many years after that I would not go back to that house. Now all is forgiven.

The next milestone in pharmacological intervention came in 1938 with the discovery of Phenytoin, the first drug specifically developed for epilepsy. It was discovered by Merritt and Putnam and is effective in controlling seizures. Again, the side effects.

Some people who take Dilantin become suicidal. Patients taking this drug are told: "*You or your caregiver should tell your doctor right away if you experience any of the following symptoms: agitation or restlessness, irritability, depression, anxiety, panic attacks, violent behaviour, withdrawing from friends and mania (an abnormally excited mood).*"

Dilantin is known to elevate blood sugar levels (increasing your risk for developing weak and soft bones) and Hodgkin lymphoma. Swelling and bleeding of the gums and gum damage are also possible. I took varying strengths of Dilantin (Phenytoin) way into my thirties and I remember how the swollen and bleeding gums tormented me. No one mentioned the side effects of medication for epilepsy so I always assumed they were as a result of some other anomaly in my body.

The 1990s saw a flurry of anti-epileptic drugs come on the market, including Felbamate and Gabapentin in 1993, Lamotrigine in 1994, Topiramate in 1996, Tiagabine in 1997 and Levetiracetam in 1999. I was prescribed Lamotrigine when I moved to Germany and was trying to get pregnant. This drug is considered a safe pre- and post- natal drug with fewer side effects than previous treatments. Taking this drug has provided me with relief, but if one reads the side effects one feels the urge to give them up. Taken directly from a R/X website I found the following side effects:

Serious skin rashes, multi-organ hypersensitivity reactions and organ failure, suicidal behaviour, aseptic meningitis, withdrawal seizures, status epilepticus and sudden unexplained death in epilepsy.

Thankfully, there are alternatives to pharmacological intervention. These include brain surgery (both invasive and non-invasive), vagus nerve stimulation and specially designed diets. The risk associated with brain surgery is high and it would certainly not be my first choice. It must also be considered that for people with epilepsy living in most parts of the developing world, brain surgery is neither accessible nor affordable.

With vagus nerve stimulation, a device is surgically implanted under the surface skin of the chest and connected to the left vagus nerve. When activated, this device sends electrical signals along the vagus nerve to your brainstem, which then sends signals to certain areas in your brain. This therapy has not had a high success rate in preventing epilepsy but is known to reduce the number of seizures. It is also not without risk, can affect the throat, heart and voice and seems to be more useful for treating depression.

The most promising and less harmful therapies seem to be the ketogenic and modified Atkins diets (MAD). These are high fat, low carbohydrate diets, primarily used to treat drug-resistant epilepsy in children and adults. The former diet requires a short period of medically supervised starvation and then an intense period of feeding with high-fat foods. A lot of work is being done on these therapies with their higher success rates of reducing seizures and leading to withdrawal from pharmo-therapy especially in children.

These diets led to the body's production of ketones which serve as an alternative energy source to maintain normal brain cell metabolism. In fact, BHB (a major ketone) may be an even more efficient fuel than glucose, providing more energy per unit of oxygen used. A ketogenic diet also increases the number of mitochondria, so called "energy factories", in brain cells. However in developing countries, it might not be possible for parents to feed their children on bacon, eggs clotted, milkshakes and similar fatty foods daily. And in countries where starchy grains are the main staple, like many parts of Africa, it seems even more difficult. So there must be alternatives.

The risk associated with cholesterol is also high for adults, although this kind of diet is associated with weight loss and not weight gain. But I would prefer high cholesterol to a seizure any day. There also seems to be some experiential logic in this type of therapy as I have observed that after a seizure. I tend to crave cream of wheat, peanut milk shakes, bacon and, of course, a KFC chicken sandwich with a large coleslaw and a chocolate milkshake.

I also remember coming home after secondary school and frying a big batch of bacon and oily chips. My body craved it.

The future for epilepsy treatment seems to be in gene therapy. It is currently being trialed in animal studies to evaluate its ability to suppress seizures along with other gene therapy experiments. Hopefully, future generations can benefit from these therapies and avoid the range of drugs and their side effects. But until that time I am grateful for the drugs even with their side effects that enabled me to go to school, get involved in community activities, study, work, be a wife and mother and enjoy a relatively normal life.

I have come to accept the fact that no one really knows why the medical community is not out there experimenting for the greater good.

But still it would be nice to know. So every once in a while (but not often) I pick up a book or search on the Internet for a clear reason why and for the cure which I have been waiting for all my life.

The truth is I don't really mind not finding a cure but I want to get off the medication. It's difficult to remember to take them and the side effects are enormous. No wonder I sleep in class, knock over everything in my wake, lose my purse or keys almost every day, forget faces and numbers and am bad at mathematics.

But guess what? I still have a little sense left in my brain to write this for those who can't. And my seizures are somewhat under control by the nasty drugs.

If you believe in demons as the cause of this suffering, that's okay. The cause does not matter; it's how one can help that makes the difference. I end this section with a quotation from the American National Institute of Neurological Disorders and Stroke (2015): "With time and continued work, the missing pieces of the puzzle will be filled in to form a complete picture of how to treat and prevent all types of epilepsy."

Casting out demons and prayer may seem the safer option and maybe I should stop wishing for a cure. I am hopeful they will find the missing piece soon. Ironically, I am blessed to be part of all these experiments.

28 After arriving back home, his disciples cornered Jesus and asked, "Why couldn't we throw the demon out?"

29 He answered, "There is no way to get rid of this kind of demon except by prayer."

WHO'S THAT?

"Tell me the number," I ask, ready to speed dial '423, 444' my mother says.

I look down at the buttons on the phone and reach out a finger and press the digit 4.

"Tell me the number again."

My mother looks at me exasperated and annunciates slowly.

4-2-3-4-4-4-4

I press the 3 and ask

4-3-2--?

"Anoush! What's wrong? I said 4-2-3…" She raises her voice slightly. "Mom, could you please write it down," I ask in frustration. I squint at it and press the numbers one by one, glancing each time at the scribbled numbers. So what exactly is the problem here? you might ask. It's simple; I have terrible memory function.

Basically, everyone has got two memory functions: short-term and long-term memory. Sensory memory is a component of short-term memory and operates to take information in. Then the rest of short-term memory process called working memory uses the information or dumps it. But you have to get the job done, like dialling a telephone number, before the information is dumped.

Long-term memory stores information over a longer time until needed.

So what exactly is my problem, you might ask. It seems to me (this is an unscientific subjective observation) that my short-term memory takes in the information and dumps it before I can use it. Or I am just daft, but can't store it.

As for my long-term memory, that takes the cake. I have a close friend who used to make fun of my poor memory function. I am sure he did not mean to be cruel. Maybe he did not think of it as a problem. We are walking down the street and suddenly someone is coming towards us and smiling as if really glad to see us. As the person gets closer I would whisper to my friend softly: "What's the name of our smiling friend coming toward us?"

My friend would burst out laughing and step back to watch me in an animated conversation to pretend to know who I am talking to. After a good long chat with our smiling friend and we parted ways and he would say: "Do you remember who it is now?" That was a rhetorical question. He already knew the answer. I didn't have a clue.

Or we would sit to watch a movie. The film would start and an actor would appear before the screen and I would say: "Wow, Mel Gibson is getting fat!"
 "That's not Mel Gibson." His lips begin to curl in a smile of superiority.
 "Sean Connery?"
 "No!" By then he is cracking up but not helping at all.
 "Denzel Washington?" (Just kidding)
 "No."
 "So who then? Please tell me who it is." I am begging now and he just laughs at my apparent stupidity.

It happens with my husband too but he is a little kinder and is not the type to torture me. But sometimes he looks at me funny. But you know what, I know the answer. I just can't retrieve a number or name from the deep dark places in the centre of my brain.

Memory deficits make life at school hell. Just imagine. The teacher asks a question: Two million plus two million. I know the answer, of course. So I stick my hand in the air. She asks John. The poor boy does not answer correctly. She asks Jane. The poor girl also doesn't calculate it right.

By then I am shouting and waving frantically because I know the answer is four million: "Please teacher, I know the answer." She turns to me finally.

 "Yes, Anoush."
 "Umm …" No words come out of my open mouth.
 "So what's the answer?"
 "Uh, what's the question again?"

Suddenly I have forgotten. I remember neither the question nor the answer. My memory has dumped the information because she has taken so long to get to me. The other children begin to laugh. I am embarrassed and the feeling lasts the whole day until I get home and get into bed replaying the scene in my mind over and over again, frustrated that I knew the answer but couldn't produce it on cue.

This deficit makes lots of things difficult: telling jokes, participating in class (I have learnt after many years to write the answer down as soon as it pops into my head), recitals and stage performances and making speeches (I am great at writing them but must read line for line when giving them). I often can't retrieve the plot or the characters of a movie or book I have seen or read. I just know I really enjoyed it. I have had many an embarrassing moment and I am certain lots of people think I am terribly stupid.

Teaching, a profession which I am not convinced I should be pursuing as a career, presents its own challenges. How to retrieve information you want to present to a class. It's hard work and I pray before every class that students don't ask me questions outside of what I have prepared. Even if I have the answer I won't be able to retrieve it. Thank God for MS PowerPoint, with all its visual cues.

The only good thing about all this trauma is that by the next morning after I have had an embarrassing moment, I have forgotten it all. Hell, my bad memory is good for forgetting.

There is scientific proof the seizures have an impact on brain function especially the hypothalamus where learning and memory processes occur. So I forget the numbers; I forget the names and I lose things constantly. I forget where I parked the car; that I put my handbag on the seat of the bus; the name of a colleague or an old friend from school.

When my daughter was born I used to be afraid I would take her somewhere and leave her there. Luckily, this didn't happen but I lost almost everything we took with us – her diaper bag, bottles of milk, her hats and so on.

So there you have it
my memory is affected
So what! That won't be recollected

A poem for you.

WHERE THE HELL ARE MY KEYS?

I have a story to tell about keys.

I am one of those lucky chaps who always lose their keys. This is not unique phenomena but somehow deep in my heart I know that when the beast is not jumping on my back. He is hiding my keys. Yes I know it sounds crazy but for someone who loses things or can't remember where they put them, losing keys is a frightening experience.

Worse yet, move from Paradise to Siberia and every once in a while the thought grips you that somehow if you lose those keys while stuck on a highway or standing outside your door on a frosty winter's day you might freeze to death. Those of you living in a cold climate or have lived at some time in wintery conditions can really appreciate this next story.

One day in the middle of winter, my lovely husband parks the car in a car park by a train station and travels to Frankfurt airport and flies across the Atlantic to the United States for a meeting.

"Oh, darling," he tells me cheerfully, "get someone to take you to pick up the car if you need it." So he leaves and I, the key loser, have to go and pick the car up.

It just so happens that over that same period, it snows heavily and the streets are blocked and dangerous to drive on. So almost three days pass, before I could go and pick up the car.

My sister-in-law, even more cheerful than my lovely husband, takes me to pick it up. As I get in her car she says to me "Let's go off on an adventure." She says this because she knows wherever I am there is some calamity. I curse her under my breath but don't bother to say anything because I am one hundred percent sure it will be fine.

So off we go chatting gaily and somewhere along the ride she says to me, knowingly: "Do you have your keys?" and I jiggle my pocket merrily and the sound of keys against each other fills the air.

Finally we reach the car park and we jump out. All around us cars are stuck in snow and some of the owners are trying to get out of parking spots. My sister-in-law has the good sense to bring along the shovel so she is running around with her cheerful self – the snow is falling on our heads, mind you – helping other people dig their cars out while I am scraping away three days of snow stuck on my car. Finally, I have cleared away enough to reach the door. I put my hand in my pocket and guess what?

No keys!

Stay calm I say to myself. Stay calm. Years of forgetting and losing things come crashing down on my head. "Barbara," I sing out cheerfully, "do you have the keys?" She looks at me with a blank expression on her face – white people are very good at that – but I can see the panic in her eyes: "Oh God, not again."

"No," she answers even more cheerfully than before, "have you checked your pocket?" She turns away ignoring me and continues to give further advice to the person she was helping to get his car unstuck.

I put my hand in my pockets. No keys. I pull the fuzz out. No keys. I check the roof of the car. I peep under it. No keys. I begin to panic and I go back to Barbara's car, who, by the way, continues to ignore me. Understandably, she does not want to be drawn into my chaos. I feel along the front seat and sides filled with panic. My husband is away so I won't be able to get in the house, I would have to leave his car and once again I would prove to his family that I am a total idiot. I looked everywhere. I shift snow – an impossible task – and I am afraid now she will drive away and leave me there to freeze to death. I am so overwhelmed I can't even remember if I had them with me or not. Maybe I had left them in the front door.

Finally she decides to have mercy and help me. She comes over smiling and we search her car together. Did I imagine her asking me if I had them? Did I really hear them jingling in my pocket? By the time I have given up, she has helped push two cars out and I am in a state of frustration. She is still smiling cheerfully. The snow starts falling again and I want to cry and we are both chilled to the bone.

We finally give up and decide that it was a stupid idea anyway because the car could have stayed there until my lovely husband came back to pick it up himself. So we sit in the car ready to leave and I run my hands one last time along the side of the seat and guess what I find? The keys.

Make no mistake, we had both searched that car each of us twice but somehow we had missed them. So I get out of her car clean the car off again and with an embarrassed thanks we part ways to do some quick shopping.

But that's not the end of it. I finally get home and go to my mother-in-law's to pick up my daughter Isabella. By then Barbara is back. Sheepishly I drag the child away from her grandmother and, because of the snow and ice on our drive way I leave my lovely red Fiesta parked near their house and Barbara takes us home.

What happens when we get there?

No keys.
I search the shopping bags.
No keys.
I pull the fuzz out of my pockets again.
No keys.
I ask poor cold and hungry Isabella if she has them.

No keys.

So Barbara says again with a blank expression but cheerfully. I'll check the car and see if I see them and bring them back. But she does not come back, believing I must have them somewhere.

We stand in the falling snow at the door of a fortress we call home: Me and my six-year-old and we can't get in. So we dump the bags and walk back down the hill to the red car.

No keys.

I am by this time brain numb and chilled to the bone. Did I park the car myself? Did I leave them in my mother-in-law's kitchen? Did I give them to Barbara? Did I even have them at all? I can't remember.

Finally, just so I don't have to admit to anyone else that I lost them, I get inside the car which is still open because in the flurry of unpacking it to get my daughter home I had forgotten to lock it. Thank God. I slide to the back and lift up the flap which separates the car from the trunk and lo and behold there are my keys sitting in the trunk of the car. So finally at 8 p.m. we make our way home in the snow.

Stupid girl, you might say. Sticks and stones may break my bones, I reply. What anyone thinks about these kinds of episodes that happen to me all the time doesn't really matter. It is not losing of the keys that's the real problem anymore, it's the fact that I am not able to remember in a crisis whether I had them in the first place. Which leads to panic that only makes matters worse.

The good news is I usually find them again.

Step on the wire and the wire won't bend. That's the way the story ends.

SCHOOL DAYS ARE HAPPY DAYS

This is a very important chapter – for all mothers and fathers, siblings with young and adult children who have learning difficulties like hearing and visual impairment, physical, emotional, behavioural and spiritual deficits; challenges of any kind. This is real life and worthy of thought.

In primary school, I was shied away from and teased like most children who are in some way "different". Children with dark beautiful skins were told how ugly they were – "Yuh black like coal"; children with severe learning difficulties were "duncy"; "She ignorant and in the duncy class"; "Boy, yuh too fat; girl, yuh real boney and bad looking" and on and on.

For my peers I was downright "nasty". Why? Because sometimes when I had a seizure, I threw up, wet myself or worse; and to top it off, I was really skinny. The result: the boys ran away whenever I walked by and the girls, though often kinder and more tolerant, sometimes followed suit just for fun. To top it off, I was the only girl in the whole school with a weird name and an afro. This added significantly to what they could tease me about.

Now I might be exaggerating. But I can only tell you what I felt at the time and when I think of my primary school experiences all I can think about are how unkind the children, especially the boys, were to me.

So what's my response to such treatment? I often went home with feelings of low self-worth and sometimes crying my little heart out. Sometimes I did not want to go back to school. I perceived their actions and words as "hate" so I hated them back and I carried my hate around with me like baggage. I could not concentrate on my school work and spent too much time in what a friend calls "mental masturbation" – thinking about what they said and did and what I could have done or said to protect myself.

Even now, decades later, whenever I visit that school just the smell of the class rooms makes me feel ill. So I stay away. While others remember the primary years with sweet nostalgia, I cringe when just thinking about it.

But please don't get me wrong, my teachers took good care of me, nursing me when I got ill at school, rubbing me down with alcolado and unfortunately sticking purses and all kind of strange things in my mouth during the attacks, so I wouldn't swallow my tongue (an old wives tale). I even had one teacher who used to make me eat, by bringing the school meals tray into the classroom after lunch period so I would be forced to eat at the beginning of class–most humiliating, but she had only good intentions.

But there also were many good days when life was fun. I found good friends and my tormentors left me alone.

When I moved on to secondary school, the teasing about the attacks stopped, partly because I was in an all girl's school and by then I was determined not to embarrass myself in front of my new class mates. I was also on new medication and my seizures where somewhat under control.

But the teasing continued for different reasons. Our music class was co-ed and the boys thought it funny that such a skinny creature with weird hair styles could have such a big butt and a flat chest. At least I no longer had that nasty girl title. I was now "A sharp, B flat". Can you guess what the A and B stand for?

So for a while I held onto the shame, anger and pain I brought with me from earlier school experiences. But that changed on a sunny day that I will remember for the rest of my life. A group of both boys and girls from my year were sitting under a huge tree at the front of the school. Those who went to Foundation back then know this tree well because it was one of the few places boys and girls were allowed to hang out together. The staff room was nearby so the teachers could keep an eye on us.

As usual the boys were giving me a hard time

"A sharp, B flat!" one of them squeezed out between his lips and everyone laughed. I held my breath, poised to flee and fighting back tears, when one of those same boys came over to me, put his arm on my shoulder saw my distress and said: "Anoush you have to chill out and not take us seriously; we are just joking around."

I remember the moment as if it were yesterday. Forty years later I even remember his name (My memory is not so bad after all.). It was at that moment that all the shame, the anger and terrible pain I had carried with me from primary school fell away and I was on my way to feeling "normal". I was still "A sharp, B flat", but at least not an object of scorn.

Quite recently, I saw one of those boys who used to torture me at primary school. He was sitting in his van in a shopping mall, so I decided to take a chance. I stomped over to the van and stuck my head through the window and asked: "Why were you all so mean to me?"

The poor man looked terribly embarrassed and ashamed and considered my question thoughtfully for a while before saying softly: "Maybe sometimes we have things we want to say but we don't know how to say them."

This shows clearly that it is really a question of perspective. What is a terrible experience for one may not be perceived in the same way by someone else. I felt persecuted and for them it was something else; but what, I am not sure. So I have had to forgive those silly little boys, in order to be free from feelings of shame, anger and low self-worth.

What I believe might help most to make school, for children who are special in some way, a positive and memorable experience is if parents, care-givers or medical professionals are allowed into classrooms to educate students about the challenges their classmates face and to engage them in discussions about their own feelings about the disability and show them how they can help.

Then "A sharp, B flat" will just be a bit of fun.

GOD BLESS MY INDEPENDENCE

There is no doubt that my parents love me. They have seen my independence and inclusion in every aspect of society as necessary and the only possibility for me to live a *normal* life.

My Dad's mission in life was to make sure I got through school and went to university and my Mum was just happy that I was well enough to live a full life.

So I was allowed to roam freely, choose my friends and get involved in social activities and go to movies, discos and parties. I choose my own career – to be just like every other child. My parents did their best to let me grow up and I am where I am today because of them. But for too long I was a child loved and protected and I found it difficult to grow up even when the opportunity for freedom, adulthood and independence presented itself.

Many persons with disabilities find themselves in situations which are crippling and destructive. As a result they have poor self-esteem and they live with phobias that they carry around like baggage. They never move away from home and often never have the opportunity to make their own decisions.

Certainly they do need some measure of protection but they MUST also be thrown out into the world early and taught how to protect themselves against teasers, users and abusers and to fight for a life they want for themselves.

It is the responsibility of parents and care-givers to ensure that their charges grow into fully independent self-actualised human beings. Push them out of the nest and let them fly.

LOVE ON A TWO-WAY STREET

A few years ago I met up with a former colleague who said he had a personal question: He was wondering why I had continued a relationship with my long-term boyfriend for almost 10 years, although it was obvious to everyone that the relationship was not working.

I'll tell you why. Safety. Security. The fear of the unknown.

When I was about 14 I went on my first date with a boyfriend. He was really a cool guy whom I liked very much and I was very proud to attend a festival with him. I remember how we wandered around looking at the things being sold in the stalls and I was very nervous and excited at the same time. Later we sat together, holding hands and smiling at each other, the way teenagers do. I think it was his first date too and we were both feeling great.

So I thought to myself, here is a smart guy, coming from the best school on the island; I am sure I can I trust him. So what did I do? I said: "I have something I want to tell you."

"What?" he answered, ready to be my all.

"I have epilepsy."

"What's that?" he asked.

"Well … sometimes I am ill…" and I began to explain carefully.

The poor boy was mortified. He stared at me with mouth opened wide and when he could finally speak, he said: "Make sure that it does not happen when you are with me or I'll slap you hard back to health!"

That was the end of my first date and whenever I go to that festival I think of that horrid day.

So now you know why bad relationships take so long to end.

Because that same boyfriend my colleague was curious about accepted my disability, watched over me and was always there for me when the beast attacked. And when finally the beast released me, this same boyfriend would scrape me up off the floor, take me home, put me in bed, wait around while

I slept, and watched TV until I recovered. He made me milkshakes and ran out to get my Kentucky chicken sandwich. But most of all he loved me still when everything was okay again.

To him it was no big deal. And I loved him for that. That's what I call real love, even in times of cholera.

Unfortunately, we eventually went our separate ways, but remain the best of friends even today.

So why did I stay?

Fear of the unknown: those who want to slap you back to health. Love, safety and security make one stay even when things no longer work.

What it takes is courage and encouragement to risk to love again. Luckily for me a certain "Fisher" man thinks it's no big deal I have epilepsy too.

CHICK AND CHILD

There is one thing I can't make fun about. Fighting of the beast, falling on my head; breaking out a tooth is not the end of the world. Dentistry has come a long way since pliers and salt water.

But the idea my only child could experience a similar attack wrecks my soul.

Motherhood is great. But no one is there to see a mother rocking that baby all night with colic and then getting up in the morning to fighting with a wayward child to put on clothes for school, comb tangled hair, and eat yucky breakfast. No one can feel her stomach coil when her teenaged daughter secretly raises the hem of her skirt to make it shorter. And what can a mother do when her son comes home with, not one but two, earrings in both ears?

No one can feel the stomach pains and heartache that crushes her the whole day after a fight with a child, second-guessing herself and wondering what she could have said or done differently.

But let's keep them in perspective.

A mother of a child who has a language deficit would be glad to be able to have a fight about clothes in the morning.

A mother with a child with a heart defect would love a healthy but colicky baby to rock at night.

A mother with a child with cancer would have relished some tangled hair to comb.

A mother with a sixteen-year-old in a wheelchair would love to see her daughter leave home for school in a short skirt.

A mother with a son with autism would love to see him come home with every body part pierced.

But what mother can be happy, can sleep well when she knows that the same beast that haunts her might turn on her baby? The mother sees the stalker even when he is not there; she waits, breath held tightly in chest, gun in hand, to shoot him should he roar.

A person with epilepsy who is also a mother, waits and waits for that beast and tries to live each day making an effort not to spend the hours watching for him. And it is on those days, after an attack that a mother lies in bed worrying that she is not able to protect her own child if the beast comes her way.

When my daughter was three years old, we were tumbling around in bed, giggling and smooching, the television was on and tele-tubbies were rolling their fat tummies and singing on screen when my daughter suddenly stopped moving and sat staring at the floor.

My heart skipped a beat. Was the beast near? There was no way for me to see him. Is he about to attack "Darling?" I passed my hand across her face. She did not flinch or move. "Darling?" I said again, taking her in my arms and suddenly she was with me again.

"Are you okay?" "Yes mummy." she answers, wrapping her arms around me tightly.

And so the torture begins. I imagine her on the ground in the school yard, the teasing and the taunting. I imagine the lost teeth, broken arms, the boyfriend who rejects her, loss of memory, problems in school. I want to try all preventative and early intervention methods out there; the cat scan and the test – the whole she-bang.

But in the end I know that I cannot control the outcome or change genetic codes.

So I hold my breath
And pray and wait
With the hope that
the beast finds her unfit bait

MIRACLES DO HAPPEN

I consider every recovery from each attack a miracle. Once the beast loses interest and looks for entertainment somewhere else. I "lie in state" until my brain decides it's time to wake up and go again. Recovery usually takes half-hour and still I spend the rest of the day and through the night in bed groggy and often with a terrible headache.

But on one special day a true miracle happened. I had been invited to the wedding of my very best friend. I was to speak on behalf of the bride. I was so excited and honoured to do this because I had waited and prayed so long for her to finally say "Yes" to the man I was sure would love and cherish her for the rest of his life..

I flew 8,000 miles to share that special moment with them, check the menu and venue (I can still rhyme), admire the cake. The day of the wedding I sat with goose pimples throughout the ceremony. After it was over the bride and groom went off to take photos and I rushed to the hotel where the reception would be held to check that everything was ready and to tuck in a few flowers.

I was rearranging a bow on a chair when that beast crept up behind me and jumped on my back. Luckily, there was a waitress nearby and I walked over to her and fell in her arms, so I never hit the ground or crumpled my chic green silk pants I had bought for the occasion. Next thing I knew I was in the arms of a strong man (I just love it) and they were dragging a sofa over for me to lie on.

The bride and groom had not yet arrived and as I lay there I stayed conscious with the thought that I did not want to spoil their day. Someone gave me some tea and, trying hard not to pass out, I asked my mum to bring me a glass of Coca-Cola. It came swiftly and I guzzled it down and sat up. I can't remember the faces of those standing around me but I remember the shock on their faces, including my mother, who kept telling me to lie down and rest.

No, I insisted, I had to get up. I must speak on behalf of the bride. I was not about to give up the opportunity to do so. I made my way to the reception hall, just as the bride and groom arrived, wobbly and nauseated, but still trying to look as *normal* as possible.

I was seated at the table with her family and all around me guests chatted and children played. Amazingly, I did not slip off my chair. My mother and the waitresses kept eyeing me suspiciously, but when the moment came for me to speak, I was lucid and all I had planned in my speech came back: what it was like when we first met and what a special person she was. I even warned her husband that he still had a lot of work to do to get into her heart and everyone agreed – she is a tough nut to crack. And everyone laughed.

I would never have forgiven myself if I had not been able to stand on that podium and speak on her behalf. But my body did not betray me and my memory did not fail me. I had given that beast a quick kick in the butt and he had run away, tail between the legs.

So miracles do happen. Thank God for Coca-Cola.

BREAKING NEWS

Lion attack in Temple Yard

I have tried to calculate how many times I have had an attack in my 48 years. Taking an average of two per year from age seven, I must have had more than 96 attacks in my life and I still have some brain cells left. I tried to think: what were the most unusual places where I fell in the claws of the beast. Both happened while I was a student at university.

The first happened when I was in my early twenties. I was at the University of the West Indies, Cave Hill campus, pursing a BA degree in History and Sociology and feeling quite smart with myself for getting so far, although I have to admit that I was not the most productive student. Maybe, too many brain cells lost.

I left campus one day and decided to go to Temple Yard. For those of you who don't know what that is, it was/is a lovely little village of workshops set up in Bridgetown, so the local Rastafarian community could make and sell their leather goods and jewelry. It was also where you could buy the most delicious ities (vegetable rotis).

No! I did not go to buy ganja, but I wanted a pair of leather sandals so I would look like a *conscious* intellectual on campus. So there I was, money in my pocket, wandering around looking at what they had to offer. I eventually found a pair of sandals I liked and stood chatting with the guy who was finishing them up for me. Somewhere along the line we got into a discussion about 'Jah' and this guy was trying to explain to me the dogma of Rasta-farianism when the discussion turned into a heated debate about religion.

I think the beast must have been lurking nearby watching us and said to himself, ah ha! she getting herself worked up and not paying attention so he sneaked up on me and wham! He was on my back, not sorry I was on my back.

The poor Rasta man must have almost had a heart attack. Eventually, I awoke and found myself in hospital. The nurses had put me on the bed and stuck me in a corner with a drip in hand. For them, and rightly so, it was no big deal. I slept and every once in a while I opened my eyes and the poor man, who had followed the ambulance on his motor bike, was sitting there watching me.

I soon got fed-up with lying there. The drip was hurting and the nurses ignored my complaints. Feeling a bit better, I took the drip out and wobbled out of the hospital.

How I got home you might be wondering. On a motor bike. My friend put me on the back of it and took me home. Can you imagine me riding on a motor bike bobbing through traffic, across Culloden Road; up Wildey, through Sargeant's Village and Vauxhall, barely hanging on to him and sleeping. We got there without me falling off. He dropped me off, relieved, I think, to get rid of me. I somehow got inside and crashed on the bed. To this day I have no idea who he was but every time one of the brethren says "Hi sister" to me, I am sure he was one of those poor guys who witnessed an attack of the beast in Temple Yard.

You are the first one I am telling this story to, but don't try this at home. It can only happen in Paradise; to the brother who took me home that day: Thanks!

The other attack was even more spectacular, however, unfortunately I don't remember much of what happened. And now I think about it it was not really funny. I was in my thirties doing my Masters Special Education at City University in New York. It was the first time I had been truly away from home and I was on my way to the university in Harlem. I was in the #3 Express train to Harlem, dog tired from studying all night and wham! the beast got me. There I was flat out on the disgusting chewing gum-covered (and God knows what else) train floor.

It seemed unbelievable and as I write this I am more and more horrified at what the poor people on the train must have gone through. Someone would have pushed the emergency button and the train would have stopped. In fact, maybe other trains must have had to stop too and the poor people on their way to work, home after night shift or taking their children to school, were stuck with me in a train. And this was in the 90s, long before anyone had cell phones.

There we were, stuck in a hot sticky train, waiting for emergency services to come.

What I do remember was what looked like a policeman standing over me screaming: "Hello; can you hear me? What kind of drugs are you on? Cocaine?" At that point I was alert and would have jumped up and whacked him one on the head if I could. "What? Are you crazy? I don't do drugs! I am just tired. Please, just take me home!"

Of course they took me to the hospital. And later I had to pay US$2,000 for a one- night stay. That's why Obama is fighting for health reform; for people like me. I thought that was a horrible experience then and too expensive but looking back I am lucky that the city of New York did not sue me for messing up the subway. Two days later, I went to the travel agent across the street and bought a ticket back to Paradise. I spent most of the flight sleeping and made it home to my own bed to rest.

Irresponsible, maybe. What do you think? Should I have just packed it in; forget about my future and stay safe in Paradise? No university! No New York City.

No way! I did go back to New York and I did get my degree. And it was where I met my husband who takes wonderful care of me.

To the people on that train. Sorry.

THANK GOD

In spite of the side effects of medication and some of the sad things that have happened in my life, I have lived with a fairly normal family life, decent sex and one healthy child (I pray still). I have had a good life and I am grateful for my blessings.

The beast may attack, I may tumble upside down, I may crack a tooth, lose some brain cells and suffer memory loss. I may traumatise others, be rejected, teased mercilessly and feel insecure.

I say sorry to all those I almost gave a heart attack; thanks to all those who love me and accept me as I am; to my parents and brother who treated me like every other parent and sibling treats the ones they love.

I say thank you to the doctors, nurses and school teachers who did not balk at the idea of being responsible for me; to co-workers and people on the street who reached out to help me; to my parents, my in-laws, my brother and other members of my extended family and friends, lovers who love me unconditionally, and to my wonderful husband who scrapes me off the floor, puts me in bed and then calmly goes back to watching football until I recover.

But most of all I thank God for his protection and for resurrecting me over and over again so I might continue to live a full life and shed some light on the very special lives of persons with epilepsy.

What I wish for most of all is that whoever is reading this little book will recognise that it is hard for individuals with epilepsy to achieve normalcy but it's not an impossible feat. I have an amazing family, life and work and live to the best of my ability.

The greatest gift that anyone can give a person with a disability is independence. The chance to live, to be, to tumble upside down and get up again and fight the beast even if one dies trying.

If life is full and rewarding then the risks are worth it. Then the disability, though ever present, becomes less problematic.

The role of family member, care-giver, teacher, neighbour and friend is to recognise that there is so much that one does not know about the special child or adult in one's care. Yet, it is important that they have every opportunity to strive for self- actualisation and independent living. So take a step back, don't bother to look for the cure; just ask: "How can I help?"

Nonpareil (excerpt)
   Why was Dan born…
   His medico didn't want to
   Sound any Claxons,
   that some of his neuronal Axons might've been lacking
   And while others got-on
   With their biz,
   Dan's state stayed dismal
   One day while playing with a mate
   He got into a state
   Paroxysmal.
   And thereafter he had to pop
   Pills that of such ills do the allaying
   The pills which would
   Pull him through
   Were blue
   And while on them he had
   To the sun eschew…
      Martin Dec. Haynes

Turn your face to the sun
Don't let people,
pills or that terrible beast leave you undone.

POSTSCRIPT

"*TESTED*" is about the lives of two remarkable women Margaret and Anoush, mother and daughter, and how they have managed their epilepsy during different phases of their lives: growing-up, as wives, mothers and professional women.

I have known Margaret for over 50 years and never knew that she suffered from epilepsy. In 1980, after the assassination of my husband Dr. Walter Rodney in Guyana I moved to Barbados with my three children Shaka, Kanini and Asha. Margaret and her two children, Anoush and Achebe, were our hosts for about two months.

During that period, and interacting as a family in fairly close proximity, I never observed Margaret having an episode. Anoush's only epileptic episode that I observed was at my daughter Kanini's birthday party. The kids were dancing and having fun when suddenly they started screaming that Anoush had fallen and was jerking on the floor. I was able to reassure them that she would be all right and they needed to give her some space since she was having an epileptic fit.

Being a registered nurse, I was able to handle this situation without causing any further anxiety to the children. I called Margaret and Colin, Anoush's Dad, came and picked up Anoush and Achebe. Margaret and I never discussed this incident and I only remember the event when I was reading Anoush's story.

The women approach the illness very differently. This may be due to their age difference and society's willingness to show more empathy towards people with different kinds of abilities. Margaret is more conformist, while Anoush is more pragmatic in her acceptance and approach. For example, they differ in the way they name the illness; Margaret describes herself as an epileptic, while Anoush views herself as someone who has epilepsy. Margaret feels victimised by the illness; Anoush is the survivor who does not give up fighting. This difference is evident throughout the telling of their stories.

Epilepsy as an illness has always been associated with personal shame; almost as if the person was responsible for this terrible affliction. It was another one of "blaming the victim" syndromes that follow people with illnesses we fail to comprehend and are afraid of, including mental illness and cancer. On reflection, was it because of the stigma associated with epilepsy that Margaret never told me about her own illness or about Anoush's?

What is it about this illness that causes ambivalence, fear and shame?
The isolation that the individual feels is often overwhelming. People often treat people with epilepsy with scant respect by either avoiding them altogether or making fun of them. This attitude is generally due to ignorance, concern and self-preservation

How many people are affected?
Globally, an estimated 2.4 million people are diagnosed with epilepsy each year. In high-income countries, annual new cases are between 30 and 50 per 100,000 people in the general population. In low- and middle-income countries, this figure can be up to two times higher. This is likely due to the increased risk of endemic conditions such as malaria or neurocysticercosis, the higher incidence of road traffic injuries, birth-related injuries and variations in medical infrastructure, availability of preventative health programmes and accessible care. Close to 80% of people with epilepsy live in low- and middle-income countries (WHO). Epilepsy can be caused by a variety of things, including stroke, brain tumour, head injury, genetics or family history. Sometimes the cause may be unknown.

Approximately 50million people currently live with epilepsy. The estimated proportion of the general population with active epilepsy (i.e. continuing seizures or with the need for treatment) at a given time is between four and 10 per 1,000 people. However, some studies in low- and middle-income countries suggest that the proportion is much higher – between seven and 14 per 1,000 people.

Social and economic impacts
Epilepsy accounts for 0.75%, of the global burden of disease, a time-based measure that combines years of life lost due to premature mortality and time lived in less than full health. In 2012, epilepsy was responsible for approximately 20.6 million disability-adjusted life years (DALYs) lost. Epilepsy has significant economic implications in terms of health care needs, premature death and lost work productivity.

Although the social effects vary from country to country, the discrimination and social stigma that surround epilepsy worldwide are often more difficult to overcome than the seizures themselves. People living with epilepsy can be targets of prejudice. The stigma of the disorder can discourage people from seeking treatment for symptoms, so as to avoid becoming identified with the disorder.

Human rights
People with epilepsy can experience reduced access to health and life insurance, a withholding of the opportunity to obtain a driving license, and barriers to enter particular occupations, among other limitations. In many countries legislation reflects centuries of misunderstanding about epilepsy.

Summary
This book provides readers with real life experiences of a mother and daughter and their unique ways of dealing with epilepsy. Despite the many setbacks and difficulties they both encountered, the women are successful in their personal and professional lives.

The book is an inspiration and can serve as a model for other people suffering from epilepsy.

Sources:
www.cureepilepsy.org/aboutepilepsy/facts.asp}
https://ufhealth97-px.rtrk.com/epilepsy-overview.Uof Florida
Epilepsy Fact Sheet, February 2016
http://www.who.int/mediacentre/factsheets/fs999/en/
https://www.nice.org.uk/guidance/cg137/chapter/Person-centred-care

Patricia Rodney, Phd, MPh